Soaring on Eagle's Wings

31 Days devotional on How Christians Can Soar to Greater Heights.

ANN-MARIE DUFFUS

Copyright © 2023 Ann-Marie Duffus
Cover copyright © by Oluwapelumi
Layout Design by Mope Sam
Editors: Mope Sam
        Editor Jane
        Amanda Hamilton-Roberts

INGS

Please note that the author's publishing style capitalizes certain pronouns that refer to the Father, Son, He, His, Him, Himself, and Holy Spirit.

ISBN: 978-9-69-339225-8 (E-book)

ISBN: 978-9-69-33226-5 (Paperback)

ISBN: 978-9-69-339227-2 (Hardcover)

For an eagle to soar "To Greater Heights" we must apply the Spiritual keys to gain strength by: Embracing Good spiritual teachings; Embracing Proper spiritual Nourishment and Vitamins by reading the Bible, praying, fasting, worshipping, spending time seeking God and abiding in His presence.

TABLE OF CONTENT

ACKNOWLEDGEMENT

I, Ann-Marie Duffus, would like to thank God for inspiring me and giving me the strength, wisdom, knowledge, and understanding to write this book. I would also like to acknowledge my kids, Oshawnie, Romario, Rovaldoe, and Collinah, who inspire me to continue holding on to God's unchanging hands. I would also like to acknowledge Mr. Davis for praying with me and encouraging me to remember that I can do all things through Christ, who gives me strength. Last but not least, I would like to thank all the leaders, intercessors, and friends who motivated, encouraged, inspired, and prayed with me through the challenging season, which gave me the tenacity to push and complete this book!

THANK YOU ALL A MILLION!

INTRODUCTION

Many people find solace and strength in the words of *Isaiah 40:31*, making it one of the most quoted verses in the Bible. This Biblical scripture has been often quoted because of the hope and consolation it offers. Putting your faith in God; patiently waiting expectantly for Him will fill you with such unshakable assurance that you will fly like an eagle through any difficulty and emerge victorious.

(Isaiah 40:31), "But those who wait on the Lord will find new strength. They will fly high on wings like eagles. They will run and not grow weary. They will walk and not faint."

In particular, the metaphor of an eagle soaring on its magnificent wings reminds Christians that they, too, may have the regal bird's fortitude, bravery, and calmness.

So, what does it mean to "soar on wings like eagles" in this Bible verse?

Isaiah urged the exiled Jews to have faith in God's promises of liberation and to wait patiently for Him to end their exile in *Isaiah 40:31*.

This kind of waiting, however, is not a passive one; rather, it is an active one. Notwithstanding their current hardships, Isaiah encourages the Israelites to wait with hope and with great confidence.

By doing so, they will be strengthened in their faith to the point that, upon God's release, they will spring from their prison cell, ready to undertake the long trek back to Judah with trust and confident certainty in God's go Eagleswings279odness. Let us dive deeper to see how this phrase, "soaring on wings like eagles," applies to you as a Christian.

Soaring on wings like an eagle is a great reminder of God's promise. As Christians, when we fail to trust Him on this journey called life, we all become weary, depressed, stressed, frustrated, discouraged, and hopeless at times, especially when waiting.

Life is a blessing whether you believe it or not. It can be glorious, but life can also be dark and dreary. It's during these dark moments God reminds us of and reassures us of His promises through His word. Waiting expectantly convinced us that He has the answer to our every need, He who gives us the strength for the moment, and whatever lies ahead.

The promises of God are true and amen. He promised that He would let us soar on wings like eagles; this soaring on Eagles Wings helps us understand God's heart towards us. This means those who trust Him wholeheartedly and have faith will rise towards heaven and above all our circumstances when we patiently wait upon the Lord. By walking in obedience to his word and listening to the voice of the Holy Spirit for directions, He blesses us with divine help and elevation through Christ.

DAY 1
SOARING ON EAGLES WINGS

The eagle is among the biggest and mightiest of all birds. A symbol of power and bravery since ancient times, the eagle has never lost its clout. The eagle served as the standard for the Roman legions throughout the years. The eagle is a universally significant emblem of leadership and success. The eagle is symbolic of strength, power, swiftness, fearlessness, concentration, bravery, and far-reaching vision.

This incredible bird prefers the cool air of the tropics. The understanding of thermal currents allows them to soar higher than any other bird.

Yet those who "wait upon the LORD" will experience a revitalization of their power and the ability to "mount up with wings as eagles," "run," and "not be weary," "walk," and "not faint," according to *Isaiah 40:31*.

What is the eagle's symbolism?

Why does Isaiah compare the Israelites' faith to that of a flying eagle? The Bible clearly uses the image of an eagle as a metaphor for something.

God likens your path of faith to that of an eagle, and to grasp this analogy, you must first get familiar with the bird itself.

Eagles are born with massive, hefty wings. Eagles extend out their wings and hold them steady to soar instead of flapping them as other birds do.

An eagle must wait for favorable conditions, such as strong wind thermals, to take off. In order to catch a wind thermal that can transport it, eagles may sometimes perch and wait for days. Because of the great wind thermals they want, eagles actively seek storms. It's prepared to weather the momentary atmospheric difficulty because it knows that, in the end, it will be projected into a calmer, clearer sky.

How Does Your Faith Stack Up Against Flying Eagles?

As a Christian, the Bible instructs that you can soar like an eagle, who uses the direction of the wind to guide his flight; you may preserve your energy by waiting on God and drawing power from Him, just as the eagle does from the wind.

Additionally, you can spread out your wings and soar with minimal effort, allowing the Lord to carry you to heights greater than you could ever attain on your own, rather than flailing your wings in an attempt to move in your own strength.

Like the eagle, those who wait on the Lord soar to great heights. They were made to fly high. That's the right spot for them.

When you put your trust in the Lord, He gives you the power you need to fly. You were meant for the pinnacles of success. You were not created to sulk in obscurity.

Because they are not used to walking or dwelling on the ground like chickens, eagles seem awkward and ungainly when they do so. Eagles are magnificent to see as they soar through the air because they were made for life in the clouds.

In the same vein, God has destined you for great success. Operating at ground level is difficult because it takes you out of your comfort zone. As it is written in the book of (*Deuteronomy 28:13*), *"If you listen to these commands of the Lord your God that I am giving you today, and if you carefully obey them, the Lord will make you the head and not the tail, and you will always be on top and never at the bottom."*

By divine promise, every child of God who follows His precepts is destined for greatness. You are destined for greatness and success. You were born to rule and soar.

Hence, stop pecking about on the ground like a chicken and start soaring like an eagle. Do not accept mediocrity. You have untapped potential for even greater success. Keep your options open. Increase the stakes; thanks to what God has already done, you have tremendous potential inside you. You can accomplish all things through Christ, who empowers you, so get started.

Eagles also have the unique ability to harness the energy of a storm for their own benefit. All other birds take cover when a storm is approaching. The eagle braves the storm on its own. An eagle doesn't fight the storm; instead, it glides calmly together with the wind. It doesn't spend its time or resources trying to outrun the storm. Rather, it positions its wings in such a manner that the winds' ferocity carries it well above the storm. When the winds pick up, the eagle soars even higher.

This implies that, as a Christian, you soar on eagles' wings through life's tempests. You soar when you listen to the Holy Spirit and do what He says.

You will soar above your storm like an eagle, when you stop fighting against the leading of the Holy Spirit and let Him lead you through your difficulties so that you might emerge victorious. Following the Holy Spirit, you won't have to fight for anything.

When you allow the Holy Spirit full control, you will soar on the wings of grace. The journey is too far for you to travel only on your own power. But if you go in the might of the Lord, you shall easily triumph. Keep in mind that as you enter an upturn and a shift, there will be adversaries. (1 Corinthians 16:9), *"For a great door and effectual is opened to me, and there are many adversaries."*

With favorable prospects, and soaring higher, there will be substantial difficulties and obligations. But you must remember that no matter what you go through, God will not abandon you. You can safely stroll across the flames without getting burned or scorched. God is with you, so even if you must go through these difficulties, you will come out stronger than before.

God intends for you to soar above the storms, like the eagle. When you are weak, you must rely on God to give you the strength you need to win.

To soar like an eagle, to run and not grow tired, and to walk and not grow faint is the privilege of those who wait on the Lord and whose daily diet consists of the nourishing words of God. This is how you choose a faith-filled, triumphant life by putting your trust in God instead of attempting to solve your issues on your own.

Don't try to manipulate the course of events to fit your schedule; instead, put your faith in God's timetable. Putting your trust in God and allowing Him to do what He knows is best will fill you with faith and hope, allowing you to reach new heights of understanding, serenity, and joy.

God wants His children to have so much joy that it spills *(John 10:10)*. Thus, if the pressures of life are pressing down on you like ominous clouds, put your faith in God and wait expectantly for a solution. And if you do, He'll fill you with such unshakable assurance that you'll be able to soar like an eagle through any difficulty and emerge victorious on the other side.

DAY 2
IT'S TIME TO COME OUT OF THE CHICKEN COOP

A coop is a compact, secure building or enclosure used to house chickens. A chicken would not want to venture outside of the coop for reasons including, aversion to change, fear of being eaten by a predator, discomfort due to the elements, or an injury. It's possible that the chickens in the run will pick on the coop-bound birds. Eagles, conversely, don't stay in the nest since they aren't scared of anything, are never too hot or cold, and never get ill or hurt.

Which word best describes you? A Chicken or an Eagle? You are an eagle, if feeling confined makes you feel like a huge chicken trapped in a little cage. Leave your comfort zone and explore the world to fully realize your abilities. Let us look at some attributes of the chicken and the eagle.

THE CHICKEN AND THE EAGLE

How is it that Christians may be crushed by the cares of this world and keep on living? This befuddles me. Day in and day out, they live with their spirits broken; only making it through life without any thought given to who they are or where they came from, and thus missing the abundant existence that is their birthright. Realizing this, I have come to the conclusion that, Christians can be divided into two species: Eagles and Chickens.

Please, I want you to utilize your creative faculties for a second. Visualize a chicken in a coop. It's foraging for food by scratching in the soil. The environment is hot, dusty, and unsanitary. Okay, now picture an eagle. It's perched high on a cliff, watching the valley below for signs of prey. Last, picture a storm brewing. On the horizon, there are some dark clouds. Heavy wind and rain are expected in a matter of minutes as thunder rolls overhead.

During a storm, what do you suppose these two birds will do? Even though they're both birds, they're taking very different approaches to weathering the storm. Both have feathers, beaks, and wings. The primary distinction between an eagle and a chicken is the way they think. What is on the inside is just as important as what is on the outside.

Despite their shared commonalities, there is a noticeable contrast between the behavioural patterns of these two species. Both have feathers, beaks, and claws, and both hatch from eggs; thus, they must be related. They share a bloodline, but fate has taken them in opposite directions. Someone is going to eat the chicken, probably with some rice and gravy on the side. The eagle is destined for great heights, where it may survey the earth below.

The achievements of the eagle are celebrated and praised. It's like the fighter jet of the avian world. As compared to other bird species, it is unrivalled in terms of altitude and speed. The Bible makes mention of these characteristics. After Saul and Jonathan were killed, David gave a eulogy in which he compared them to the eagle, saying, *"Saul and Jonathan were gorgeous and delightful in their lives...they were swifter than eagles"* (2 Samuel 1:23). The eagle is held in high regard for its impressive flight capabilities. Its massive wings allow it to reach incredible heights and do fantastical feats. Hence, the capabilities of the eagle's wings are a representation of our God.

The eagle's exceptional maternal care for her offspring is only one of its endearing traits. No other bird is more tender-hearted or caring toward its young. It constructs its nest atop a precipitous outcrop of rock. Both parents feed the young eaglets, and they are all involved in the process of learning to fly. If the youngster becomes too tired to continue flying after taking off from such a great height, the eagle will swoop down and carry it on its wings.

As God carried His people "on eagles' wings," the eagle stands as a symbol of His dealings with His people.

Do you ever observe a chicken's daily routine? Chickens are always foraging in the yard, strutting their feathers, and scratching in the dirt. Searching through trash cans for unwanted leftovers. Scratching and gazing, looking and scratching... Chickens are so curious that I'm willing to wager they'd tell you anything if you asked them.

Yet you will never find an eagle doing yard work. An eagle will not consume a carcass; the eagle won't eat anything he doesn't kill himself. The eagle won't receive any charity from any bird; they are self-sufficient.

Chickens flock together, from sleeping to foraging to brooding their young together. An Eagle is never found chatting it up with other Eagles. An Eagle will eject its offspring when the time has come for them to mature and leave the nest.

I want you to realize that the spiritual realm mirrors the physical one. Some persons you encounter are confident in their identity as Christians. In contrast, other Christians are not attending to the Father's affairs; the world remains blissfully unaware of their existence. Such people carry the weight of the world on their shoulders as they plod through life. They give the impression of being hopeless because of their domestic and professional situations, their children's behavior, and their partners' absence. They believe the Devil's lies that they are weak and insufficient.

If you come to terms with the reality that you are God's child, that you were made just slightly inferior to the angels, and that your Father owns all the livestock on a thousand hills, you will recognize that you are meant for grandeur.

In the beginning, while God was making the world, after making sure it was fit for human habitation, He got down on His knees in the dirt and formed humans. Then when He looked at you, He said, "Excellent," giving you His seal of approval. Yet, between then and today, you have managed to completely screw things up... You have let the enemy fool you into believing his falsehoods about you. You fool yourself into thinking that you are a minority and are destined to make do with the world's scraps.

According to the Bible, God will never look upon His offspring grovelling for food. He promises to take care of us completely and never abandon or leave us. So, you must make up your mind to leave the chicken coop because that is not where you are meant to be.

I would like to conclude this section with an inspiring story:

"Once upon a time, there was a great hillside on which an eagle's nest perched. There were four big eagle eggs in the nest. During a particularly violent tremor, one of the eggs rolled all the way down the mountain to a chicken farm in the valley far below. The hens understood they were responsible for safeguarding the eagle's egg, and one elderly hen stepped up to take on the task.

The egg hatched, and the baby eagle was a sight to behold. The eagle, sadly, was trained to kill chickens. Within a short timeframe, the eagle had come to see himself as little more than a chicken. The eagle deeply appreciated eagles when they soared; not knowing they were his real family, his heart always yearned for adventure.

A trio of powerful eagles was soaring above the farm one day when the eagle looked up from a game he was playing. The eagle wished it could fly as well as other birds. The elderly hen came and told him, "You can't fly with the eagles. You can't fly because you're a chicken."

The eagle kept peering up at his true family, wishing he could join them. Every time the eagle shared his hopes and goals, he was met with rejection.

The eagle had internalized this wrong belief. The eagle eventually gave up dreaming and resumed his mundane chicken-like existence. The eagle, who had been living as a chicken for quite some time, eventually died and never lived to his true potential.

Don't be like this eagle; remember that you are what you say you are. Therefore, if you want to soar like an eagle, don't listen to a chicken telling you to land like one.

There is a popular saying by *Henry Ward Beecher, "You are not called to be a canary in a cage. You are called to be an eagle and to fly sun to sun, over continents."*

Let me tell you a testimony of how God delivered me from the chicken coop through the power of Jesus Christ. I am Prophetess Ann-Marie Duffus. I have been saved for more than 15 years. I am a chosen, appointed, and anointed vessel of God. I am an eagle, but I felt like a chicken that has been locked into a chicken coop for years.

I was limited by witchcraft and marine powers. I remember on Wednesday night, February 16, 2022, at 8:30 p.m., I went on Facebook on a Live that was being hosted by Prophetess Minlin Coleman, the wife of Pastor Marvin Coleman, the founders of Mended Vessels Christians Community Church in Queens, New York. I remembered she was moving by the gift of prophesy. At that time, she acknowledged me by my then Facebook name, "Annie Bless."

She started prophesying by the leading of the Holy Spirit; she said, "Annie Bless, I see where you should have been further than where you are now, but you have been limited for years, and in a stagnant state. I need you to type the correct name that you were given at birth." I typed my name Ann-Marie Duffus on the screen, and then Prophetess Coleman said, "I see in the realm of spirit where a passport has been locked up in a box and buried for you, and it has been the altar that is connecting you to the kingdom of darkness." Then she instructed me to purchase a gold and white prayer shawl and send me on a seven (7) days prayer and fasting. I did as I was instructed.

Five months later, on Thursday, June 16, 2022, in the community of Temple Hall, Kingston, Jamaica, where my house is located. I received a call from a contractor that was currently working on the house at that time. He said, "Dubbie wah gwaan!" In a very loud voice (the pet name by which I am called). "Lawd gad! Mi deh yah a wuk eno and yuh know seh mi find yuh old passport inna di fowl(chicken) coop, lock-up inna a box, bury betwizt (between) two piece a board." Then he went further to say, "If dah fowl (chicken) coop yah neva mash-up, yuh woulda neva know seh sinthing bury yah so!"

A few months later, The Holy Spirt told me to visit Mended Vessels Christians Community church in Queens, New York, and God used the leaders and intercessory team to pray for me and deliver me from bonds of wickedness in Jesus' name. Amen!

I shared this testimony with you to encourage and inspire you, not to let the enemy limit you, don't stop at the chicken coop. I was limited and held back from maximising my full potential, walking into my purpose, and soaring on the wings of an eagle. Like I was, many persons out there today have been limited, and the spirit of stagnation is upon them, but the Holy Spirit leads me to write this devotional to inspire you. May every chicken coop you have locked up in be broken down from around you, and the eagle in you shall rise to maximise your full potential and fulfill your God-given destiny in Jesus' name. Amen!

DAY 3
CREATE AN EAGLE MINDSET

The mind is everything in a human being. Your thoughts are a direct product of your mind, and your actions are a reflection of what goes on in your mind. Your overall productivity and performance quality is a function of your mindset. The truth is, if you think right, you act right. Therefore, you must understand how the human mind works and affects our daily living.

What are Mindsets? Mindsets are mentalities; a person's mentality may be defined as their collection of self-aware ideas and beliefs. These set the stage for how people act, think, and feel. An eagle's mindset is how eagle's think, act and feel; this will be our discussion here. I will start by telling another inspiring and interesting story.

There was once a farmer who stole an eagle's egg from its nest. He brought it home and put it beneath one of his hens, and soon a little clutch of chicks emerged. The farmer patiently sought to grow and tame the bird. The eagle was always a little out of place among the hens. It never walked with the flock, preferring to go its own way, and ignoring the hens.

As the eagle matured, he began to suspect that something was amiss on the inside. While he had never known anything else, the chicken yard never felt like a rightful place of refuge. He desired to escape the coop and soar over the clouds.

The eagle even attempted to get away, but the farmer clipped his wings to blocked him from taking off. The eagle was unable to fly, so he spent his days sitting in the chicken yard and staring at the sky. The sky darkened as a storm approached one day, sending the barnyard animals scrambling for shelter. The chickens, being chickens, were understandably terrified.

The eagle rested and observed his surroundings, knowing the storm held no fear for him. He felt compelled to spread his wings then and discovered that the farmer had neglected to trim them. A magnificent eagle, its wings spread in a regal display, appeared in his peripheral vision, soaring on the wind above him.

Once more, the eaglet that had been reared as a chicken gazed about at the other chickens running around wildly, then looked up at the eagle flying serenely above him. An impressive, eerie screech from the eagle reached his ears. At that same moment, he realized he had to get the heck out of that coop! A powerful wind current surged beneath his spread wings, carrying him aloft. He screamed his way out of the barnyard with a sense of triumph and independence.

YOU MUST HAVE AN EAGLE'S MINDSET

It is crucial that you have an eagle's perspective and never give up on your goals. I told you the story of the eagle in the chicken yard to inspire you to be who you are and make the bold decisions necessary to set yourself free from anything that is keeping you from realizing the grandeur for which God created you to be.

Is there ever a time when you feel like an eagle in a henhouse? You are aware that you have much more potential than you are currently allowing yourself to tap into and express. God has a wonderful plan for your life, and you feel an irresistible pull to fulfill it. Do you realize that to fulfill God's plan for your life, you will have to put in long hours, risk failure, face isolation, let go of possessions, make tough choices, and maybe face criticism and rejection?

Keep in mind: No eagle ever felt at home in a stable. They're all homesick for the wide-open spaces of a desert. It's natural to feel uneasy when residing in a setting that prevents you from being true to yourself and fulfilling your purpose in life.

Pay heed to the stirrings of your heart, spirit, and intellect when the idea of going further than where you are begins to take root, when a seed of greatness begins to develop, and when you feel a strong need to take a risk and try something new. Go forward with it. Yet you should also be aware that your peers might not share your enthusiasm for unconventional thinking. They could try to stifle you. They could even tell you, "Now calm down and act like the rest of the chickens. Here we have a pleasant chicken coop with tasty grubs and worms."

When you have it, why would you want anything else? When confronted with such inquiries and comments, you may wonder, "What's wrong with me?" Why do I think the way I do? Why do I get this feeling? Why can't I stop trying to change the world and just live a regular life like everyone else? You are not a chicken; you are an eagle, so you cannot simply relax.

You were meant for more than that chicken yard can offer, and you will never find true contentment there. Today, I want you to stoke the fire that's already within you. That fire is burning deeply on the inside. Keep it aerated until it burns brilliantly. Have your sights fixed on the greatness you were designed for, embrace your individuality, and never let anyone tell you that you can't achieve your goals and fulfill your God given purpose. Understand that your yearning for exploration is a divine gift, that your curiosity about new things is a fantastic trait, and that living fully and reaching for the stars is what you were created to do. An eagle, you are!

There are lots of eagles that think they are chickens for many years. This is a serious issue since eagles that mistake themselves for chickens will act like chickens. Instead of calmly and elegantly soaring above the storms, they would scratch and flutter around the barnyard, creating a lot of noise.

"As he thinks in his heart, so is he," the Bible declares, revealing a profound truth about the mind (Proverbs 23:7). What you think about, you bring about. You will end up being the product of your own thoughts, priorities, and environments. As a storm approaches, a bird will react with panic and hysteria if it believes it is a chicken, but it will show strength and bravery if it believes it, is an eagle.

I have some fundamental questions for you, and I want you to give thoughtful, forthright answers. Just how do you feel about yourself? How do you rate your own self-worth? In what ways do you view yourself? Are you proud of who you are? Do you find it difficult to connect with your own self? Do you spend more time alone or with other people? You can never truly escape from yourself. No matter how hard you try, you can never escape your own company in this world. That's why it's crucial to respect and like oneself, to feel good about who you are.

I believe that individuals in many cultures worldwide, are experiencing a crisis of self-respect because they are not prioritizing their health and well-being. Some people even consider placing oneself last a sacred act. They believe God expects them to put everyone else's needs before their own and give up all for the sake of service.

Certainly, we are commanded to be selfless, to give of ourselves, to put the needs of others before our own, and to shun avarice and selfishness. On the other hand, we are tasked with accepting the reality that we are the individuals in whom God resides. Taking care of ourselves is an act of worship because we are His, He wants to use us, and we are the sort of people that make others want to know Him.

You are the abode of Christ *(1 Corinthians 6:19)*. You are His dwelling place; He inhabits your whole being. If you overcommit, overwork, eat junk food, don't get enough water, sleep, or relax, and don't exercise, you will demolish the temple and become spiritually malnourished. Also, you will become spiritually obese. You won't be doing yourself, others around you, or God any favors if you're always sick and exhausted. You won't be able to make it through the bad patches or appreciate the good moments to their fullest.

From this day on, please treat yourself with the utmost dignity and compassion by attending to your emotional, mental, physical, and spiritual needs.

Practice self-control by getting enough shut-eye, eating right, drinking lots of water, and working out regularly. The positive effects on your state of mind, emotional stability, and physical vitality may take you aback. The eagles always have vitality.

You should always think that you have the makings of an eagle. God wants you to be an "Eagle Christian," someone who can soar above the difficulties of life and still have a calm, confident demeanor despite of the turbulence around you. You need to start seeing yourself the way God does. Get started by appreciating yourself because He appreciates you. Leave behind your "chicken attitude and mindset" and soar like the eagle you truly are.

DAY 4

CREATING A MENTALITY TO LIVE YOUR REALITY

In the last section, we talked about having an eagle mentality because it helps every Christian live their reality.

God is attempting to teach us something when He likens us all to eagles in this verse *(Isaiah 40:31)*. When I first read this line, it leaped right off the page and into my mind.

I studied eagles and their personalities a few years ago to see if there were any qualities intrinsic to the eagle that God wanted us to have in our relationship with Him.

After learning more about the characteristics eagles actually possess, I came to the conclusion that God was attempting to teach us something about the things He values most in human beings. This is a strong and meaningful parallel, and it applies to every Christian. Let's get right into it.

If you want to get the essence of the eagle's analogy, you need to comprehend the fundamentals of eagles' flight, which focuses mostly on the bird's ability to soar without flapping its wings.

Their wings are completely extended and appear to be floating effortlessly on the air currents.

Eagles have to develop the ability to fly without flapping their large, heavy wings; this is a necessary adaptation for their species.

Therefore, eagles must learn early on, to wait for wind thermals to come upon them to soar without beating their wings. Thermal wind is a powerful upwards-moving wind gust.

It can take an eagle days of waiting for the perfect wind conditions before taking off, but once they do, they can use a combination of flying and soaring on the powerful wind thermal to bring them wherever they need to go.

This is the reality that God expects every Christian to work in. The key point of this comparison is that God is providing us with a tremendous illustration of how eagles fly and soar on these wind thermals. What do eagle, eagle wings, and wind thermals signify, and how can they help you to live your reality?

The Eagle signifies you.

The Eagle's wings symbolize faith and trust in God.

The Wind thermals symbolize the Holy Spirit.

According to this verse, God's message and your reality in this world is that it is the Holy Spirit's power working through you, not your own, that will help you fulfill His plan.

Like the eagle, you, as a Christian who has been born again and filled with the Holy Spirit, must learn to rely on the indwelling of the Holy Spirit to propel you through life. To put it another way, you need to train to walk and fly in God's anointing.

The anointing of God is the Holy Spirit's presence inside and power exerted through you to execute God's will on earth. When compared to God, your strength is diluted and restricted. It would be best if you learned how to soar on the wings of the Holy Spirit.

Learning to follow the Holy Spirit's guidance and to move in step with His anointing is essential if you are to work in your reality and fulfil every aspect of your divine destiny for the Lord.

You will never know the specifics of God's plan for you to serve Him in this life until you train yourself to follow the Holy Spirit wherever He may lead you.

In this lifetime, you will never meet your real soul mate or accomplish the purpose for which God created you if you are not led and moved by the Holy Spirit.

Just as the eagle must learn to ride and navigate on those wind thermals once it actually launches into them, learning to walk with the Holy Spirit's power functioning through you is crucial if you are to properly complete the tasks and assignments God will be calling you to undertake in this life.

In order to do the exact things God will call you to perform for Him, you need to learn how to be led by the Holy Spirit. However, if you don't also learn how to walk and flow with His actual power, you will fail miserably.

The eagle's wings stand for your trust and confidence in the Lord. In the end, nothing will change unless you develop sufficient trust in God to soar on the wings of the Holy Spirit, where you shall be guided and enabled to serve the Lord to your full potential.

If you don't trust God, you will remain in your current position, never realizing the potential God saw in you before you were conceived.

The only way for the eagle to take advantage of the wind thermals is to take a giant jump from the cliff. The eagle will starve to death atop the cliff if he does not take advantage of the wind thermals that periodically rise up to meet him.

Just as the Bible says God's people will be destroyed if they do not have His precise vision for their life, so too will your life be destroyed before your own eyes if you do not take flight on the Holy Spirit and the divine call that God has placed on your life.

If you have decided to devote your life to walking in your reality and service to the Lord, you will hear God calling you, and you will have to learn to fly by jumping from a cliff.

The only thing that will allow you to soar on the reality that God has placed on your life is your faith, obedience, and confidence in the Lord, just as the wings of the eagle are the only thing that will allow it to fly and soar on those wind thermals.

You are the eagle; your faith, obedience, and trust in the Lord are your wings, and the Holy Spirit's presence and strength are the wind thermals that propel you toward realizing your entire divine destiny for the Lord.

DAY 5
THE POWER OF PIVOT

The only constant thing is change itself, which means that change is inevitable. You have the ability to alter your behavior at any moment and under any conditions. Don't settle for where you are in life right now. Whether you're getting paid for your job or not, creative careers go through cycles, and one of those cycles is pivoting.

Everyone reaches a turning point at some point in their lives. A turning point is a defining moment in one's life that can lead to significant personal growth and development. If you are summed up, how will you know if you have succeeded or failed, and to what extent? This is the Power of Pivot; you will delve into the idea that the key to achieving out-of-the-ordinary success lies in how you respond at turning points in your life, not just in terms of what you do but also in terms of what you say, think, and feel. It's all about becoming increasingly valuable, responsible, and relevant to yourself and the society at large.

In the book of Romans 8: 28 – "And we know that in all things God works for the good of those who love him, who have been called according to his purpose." Much can happen through the "Power of Pivot," but you must have a positive mindset that God is working out everything for your good. The Power of Pivot allows the Will of God to happen into your life.

The transformation of an unsatisfying work environment into a more satisfying one, a stagnant sales process into a productive sales funnel, being an unfruitful Christian to a more fruitful Christian, or changing one deal into another is only part of the Power of Pivot. How you accept the pivot, how you think about it, how you absorb it, and how you decide to deal with the shift in course is what gives you the power.

The world around us is always evolving; no matter how tough you think you are; you can't ignore that reality. And you have a choice to adapt to the new realities or remain permanently mired in the past.

The Adaptive Trait of an Eagle

In order to survive to be 70 years old, the eagle must make a difficult choice in its forties.

Its long, pliable talons are no longer effective enough to catch the food it needs to survive and its long, pointed beak kinks. The thick feathers on its aging wings cause them to stick to the animal's chest, making flight difficult.

The eagle then has two options: die or undergo a painful transformation lasting 150 days. The bird must then fly to a mountain, repeatedly striking its beak on a rock until the talons become loose enough to be plucked.

At this point, the eagle will have to wait for its beak to regrow. Within 5 months, the eagle can take its rebirth flight and lives another 30 years once its new talons have grown back and it has begun plucking its old, ragged feathers. This is the power of pivot because pivoting leads to tremendous transformation.

Starting a process of transformation is often necessary for survival. It's important to shed the baggage of the past; only when your past is no longer shackled can you fully enjoy your present.

The eagle is an expert at adapting to new situations. The eagle mother builds a cozy nest for her eggs. When it's time for the eaglets to learn to fly, the mother starts taking away the soft bedding and exposes the sharp sticks and twigs. The eaglets watch as she tosses them from the nest. She keeps doing this repeatedly until the Eaglet master's flight.

The eaglet is too scared to leave the nest, so it keeps diving back in, each time screaming and getting poked by the nest's sharp edges. There is no giving in from the mother eagle. This may seem heartless to onlookers, however, there's a logic behind all this chaos. The procedure is continued until the eagle begins beating its wings, gaining strength with each beat.

Then... whizz! It takes off into the sky and rises rapidly in altitude, overcoming obstacles and suffering. The lesson of life is that you must resist the urge to settle into a comfortable rut. Only by challenging yourself outside of your safe habits can you expect to develop. Life's thorns and bruises are there to teach you two important lessons:

1. That you have reached the end of your current potential.

2. That it is time to advance, develop, and extend your wings.

Individuals who genuinely care about you won't support you while you wallow in laziness and terror. The way they will treat you may not appear nice, but it is in everyone's best interest. It's important to show affection, but there are moments when it has to be stern. They don't want you to perish in your nest!

As Christians we represent the life of an eagle. There comes a point in one's life where you have to make changes, in order to soar higher! There's power in pivoting.

DAY 6

THE POWER OF BEING A FAITH WALKER

When you think of an eagle in flight, what do you picture? You picture a lone bird soaring against a clear blue sky. Eagles are typically seen as solitary birds, not in groups. It's because eagles prefer to fly alone.

They don't travel in groups like geese or quail do when they fly. In the United States, the month of October marks the departure of thousands of swallows from San Juan Capistrano, California, while March marks their return. Together, these birds travel the "group trip" from California to their wintering grounds in the southern United States every year in the spring. A flock of larks, chirping or singing together, is something you might encounter, but a flock of eagles is something you won't.

They never go anywhere in packs. The eagle has the character of independence and the spirit and power to soar on its own.

The first thing you need to realize if you are going to become an "Eagle Christian" is that there will be moments when you have to do it alone. Taking an alone flight is a leap of faith. The faith's first pioneer, Abraham, was singled out and sent on his journey without anybody else. Becoming a person of faith requires practice in solitude.

This fact does not preclude the possibility of romantic or platonic attachments. This merely implies that you will frequently be put in a position where you must make and implement choices that set you apart from the crowd and allow you to soar further than your peers would be interested in attempting.

At one point, I was griping about how alone I was, saying, "I don't have any friends. It feels like I never see anyone." People often label me as eccentric and fanatical. Some members of my own family no longer have any affection for me. God's Spirit whispered to my soul, telling me to remember this fact: other birds travel in groups, but eagles soar above the clouds on their own.

As an "Eagle Christian," you can expect to face periods of isolation. To walk by faith means there will be times when you must go alone, whether as a parent or at work, and you will need to act on your convictions despite the pressure of others to do otherwise.

Perhaps it might be the thought of telling your boss a little white lie or giving in to the urge to "fudge the numbers." Defending your kids' best interests often requires you to go alone as parents because all your son's friends may be unsupervised as they play violent video games or surf the internet.

Being a faith walker could mean you will refuse to join a group activity or social gathering. It's possible, that you will be required to forego a social gathering in favor of some alone time with God. There is nothing inherently wrong with skipping the party to spend quality time with God and renew your attitude. In fact, to fly like an eagle and walk by faith, you might have to forego the party.

It's possible that the Lord will have you switch careers. This isn't because the first one was bad for you but because He wants you to learn to put your faith in Him rather than in the success of your own efforts.

In any of these scenarios, you may need to take a position and ignore the opinions of those around you. The tougher option might be setting limitations with your kids or co-workers. The idea of spending alone time in prayer and Bible study may not appeal to your enthusiasm. But you and the people you care about will benefit from the confidence and clarity that comes from a life lived by faith. The knowledge that you have obeyed God rather than acting on your own whims will also bring you great comfort. This is the benefit of walking by faith.

Being a person of faith doesn't mean you never get tired or stressed out; it means that when you do, you turn to God and let Him renew your strength. Spending extra time with God when you feel fatigued creeping in could save you from losing your tempers or saying things you later regret. You will be encouraged to keep going and not give up.

Don't stop short of discovering and appreciating who you are, encourage yourself to become and accomplish everything God has for you. Never lose hope in God's plan for your life, no matter how much you may feel like an eagle among hens. Even though you know your flaws inside and out, don't let that stop you.

Don't let your problems keep you from God; take them to Him. He alone can aid in your triumph against them. Do not give up because of your own shortcomings; we all have them. Don't be too hard on yourself if you falter along the way; instead, quickly return to God. Keep in mind that your shortcomings do not take God aback. He foresaw them long before you did, and He still loves you, continue walking in faith, and you will see yourself soaring.

DAY 7
THE POWER OF BEING OBEDIENT TO GOD'S WORD

Accepting God's authority and instructions humbly and sincerely is essential to being obedient. It's more than just following the rules; it's showing your allegiance with your words and actions.

To get to know God, to have an intimate relationship with Him, you must submit to Him. Without obeying the Lord, however, there is no way to draw near to Him, take full advantage of His blessing, or experience the communion your soul longs for.

To have a close relationship with Him and to reap the reward of that relationship, you must walk with Him, obey His Word, and follow the direction and leadership of the Holy Spirit. Soaring to greater heights of the spirit and walking with God is possible only through obedience. Below are some of the benefits of being obedient.

1. Obedience is a prerequisite for a relationship with God. Take a look at these Old Testament characters that had a wonderful relationship with the Lord and see how their obedience shaped that relationship.

I. Enoch

"Enoch lived in close fellowship with God" (Genesis 5:22) for three hundred years, according to the Bible. Consider the benefits to your soul and spirit of spending 300 years on earth in intimate communion with the Lord, listening to His voice, learning His methods, and caring for the things that matter most to Him. That is how Enoch lived. Which leads to what?

According to the Bible, Enoch did not die a physical death. Instead, God *"took him" (v. 24), and "he disappeared."*

II. Noah

Noah's life was a difficult one. There was so much evil in the world, the Bible says, that *"the Lord was sorry he had ever made [humanity]" (Genesis 6:6).*

Then He declared, *"I will destroy every last trace of the human race I created. Yes, and I will wipe out all life (v. 7)."* There had been a period of desolation, yet God took notice of Noah. That *"Noah found favor with the Lord" (verse 8).* As opposed to adopting the immorality of his culture, Noah promoted virtue. Noah and his family were spared from the flood that wiped out all other life on Earth because he obeyed God. Other people in the Bible also had a pleasant experience in their walk with God because of Obedience.

2. Obedience allows you to hear and respond to God's voice. Many nice and charitable individuals in the world do not have a personal relationship with the Lord and, as a result, are deaf to His call. On the other hand, as a Christian, you have the privilege to hear God and act accordingly. His children have the right to His voice, and His voice and character are made known to us through the Bible, the Holy Spirit, and the counsel of other Christians (such as leaders in the faith, role models, prayer partners, friends in the faith, etc.).

According to (*Deuteronomy 4:5-6*), *"You must obey these laws and regulations when you arrive in the land you are about to enter and occupy. The Lord, my God, gave them to me and commanded me to pass them on to you. If you obey them carefully, you will display your wisdom and intelligence to the surrounding nations. When they hear about these laws, they will exclaim, 'What other nation is as wise and prudent as this."*

When you obey and respond to God's leading, you will demonstrate His wisdom to the world, which may lead some of them to believe in Him.

3. Obedience makes you fortunate.

If you obey God, He says, good things will come to you. Take a look at these scriptures to see how God rewards those who are obedient to Him:

(Joshua 1:8), "This Book of the Law shall not depart out of your mouth, but you shall meditate on it day and night, that you may observe and do according to all that is written in it. For then you shall make your way prosperous, and then you shall deal wisely and have good success."

(Isaiah 1:19), "If you are willing and obedient, you will eat the good things of the land."

Even though God loves and favors all His children, it is obvious from scripture that obedience usually comes with a special reward, so it is important that you are obedient to God's word.

4. Obedience to God's word help you put your faith in God.

To obey God is to make room for God to work in your life through His Word, His Holy Spirit, and His manner of doing things. Believe that He will keep His promises. When you submit and obey Him, you stop relying on your own abilities to shape your life and the world around you. Instead, you keep your eyes on the Lord, meditate on His Word, submit to His will, and rest assured that He will do what He has promised.

To say you adore God while rejecting His commands is a lie. Make a pact to obey Him out of genuine affection for Him and gratitude for what He has done for you. The God you serve is enormous, magnificent, and totally awesome. Instantly and completely obey Him so that you may walk closely with Him and reap the rewards of your obedience.

In our foundational passage *(Isaiah 40:31)*, Isaiah uses an image of an eagle, not only of bodily growth, to describe the journey we walk with God. The image of an eagle signifies that there will be spiritual peaks where your connection with God soars.

There will be occasions when God gives you the green light to journey ahead. However, this journey is just one lengthy line of many orders to come, heading in the same direction. It's true that you will be travelling a long way on a rough path. There are mountains and valleys along your path through which you will journey. It's characterized by broken pavement and epidemics. You will be tired from the long travel ahead of you; however, those who obey and put their trust in the Lord will find renewed vitality. The Lord will bring home those who obey him.

DAY 8

RELEASE YOUR PRAISE

The Psalmist says in *(Psalm 16:11), "In thy presence is fullness of joy; at thy right hand there are pleasures for evermore."*

Eagles have been revered as a symbol of strength, nobility, grace, and masculine virtues by men for centuries. The qualities of this bird make it a powerful emblem for all people, and the eagle's ability to harness the power of a storm is just one example of this.

The only birds who like a good storm are eagles. When a storm is brewing in the distance, an eagle will know it. The bird then soars to a lofty vantage point to await the arrival of the winds. When storm clouds gather and the sound of thunder rolls and echoes throughout the sky, the eagle takes off. When an eagle is caught in a storm, the air currents carry it high above the storm due to the eagle's wing position. While most birds seek safety, run away, or hide during a storm, eagles soar straight into the eye of the storm and ride the winds to greater heights.

They take advantage of the storm's pressure to rise effortlessly. Their ability to lock their wings in a fixed posture in the middle of severe gusts is a special gift from God. The eagle is then carried higher by the wind. That's why you will see the eagle soaring high above the raging storm. The more intense the storm, the higher the eagle flies.

And like the eagle, you can use life's storms to your advantage. When you let the Holy Spirit carry you through your difficulties, you are able to rise above them. God's Spirit can transform obstacles into springboards that launch you into your full potential.

So, do not be disheartened but rather be glad and rejoice in the midst of adversity, for you know that God is able to make way for you, even through the huge seas.

Even if you don't have all the answers and don't know how to proceed when a storm hits you, you will never have to fight for anything if you seek God's guidance and follow the promptings of the Holy Spirit.

You can soar higher with God and reach more expansive shores like the eagle. You should get closer to God in difficult circumstances because He always knows how to turn things around.

Victory in combat depends on your ability to always keep God's presence with you. To draw God into your midst, you must always glorify Him by releasing your praise. When you sing praises to God, He awakens, and His enemies scatter.

When King Jehoshaphat faced an overwhelming army, he did not rely on his own might but instead sought out the presence of God through worship (2 Chronicles 20). When God is with you, there is no way you can lose a fight.

Therefore, take heart in knowing that difficulties merely fortify your character and not turn you sour. Like the eagle, you can use the storm to your advantage and soar to new heights. The purpose of adversity is to fortify you and bring you closer to God. Because of this, even the tough times are considered good experiences. The praise you release serves as a catalyst for entering God's presence, where complete joy can be found.

The words "in thy presence is fullness of joy; at thy right hand there are pleasures for evermore" will be fulfilled in your life and situation when you release your praise.

As long as you keep praising God, you will completely triumph over your enemies because God is with you, and victory belongs to you.

DAY 9

THE ENEMY HAS PUT A FULL STOP TO YOUR LIFE, BUT GOD IS GETTING READY TO BEGIN A NEW SENTENCE

Do you believe that flying is an illusion? Have you given up because no matter how hard you try, you always seem to fail? Do you believe that you have reached the end of the road? Do you believe the enemy has sabotaged your life to the point where you are a mere apparition of who you once were? Do you think you have lost your strength and can't soar to new heights anymore?

The moment you think you have reached your limit, God begins a new sentence and a new chapter with you. Don't listen to the falsehoods of the enemy; instead, shift your perspective and seek God's vision. *In Isaiah 43: 19 – "For I am about to do something new. See, I have already begun! Do you not see it? I will make pathway through wilderness. I will create rivers in a dry wasteland."*

What has Satan done to you that a shallow place of mediocrity feels like your final resting place? God is currently altering the situation right now; He does not see things the way you see them. He sees life when you see death. He sees health when you see sickness. He sees hope when you see hopelessness.

The enemy's goal is to steal, kill, and destroy whatever good you have in the world, and he does this by convincing you that your life is in shambles and that the end has come.

Know that God gives life abundantly to anyone who comes to Him, since God is the source of life. The devil has implanted a false belief in your mind to stop your life. You must free yourself from these falsehoods, false beliefs, false hope, and faulty mindsets because they are the anchors that prevent you from reaching new heights. God wants to begin a new sentence in your life; he wants to do a new thing in your situation. You have to trust Him, having faith in the plans that He has for you.

Have you seen an eagle soar with a heavy weight on its wings? Eagles are carried by the strength of the wind; thus, anything that would make them too heavy would prevent them from taking flight. This is how difficult it will be for you to soar if you don't take away all the wrong mindset and heavy loads that the enemy has used to hold your life.

If you want to soar above the clouds as an eagle, you need to clear your head of all the erroneous ideas and evil thinking that are keeping you grounded. It's crucial to renew your mind through God's word after you've cleared it of erroneous ideas. As we continue this devotional, we'll talk more about how to experience a rejuvenated mind.

DAY 10

TRUST THE PROCESS IN SPITE OF WHAT YOU SEE BEFORE YOUR EYES

Having faith in the process and refusing to give up does not imply squeaking by each day with no reserves of energy or happiness. A person who refuses to give up exudes a special type of strength, experiences a special kind of victory, enjoys a special kind of triumph, and is driven by a special sort of enthusiasm. A person with such willpower, resilience, and ability to overcome adversity can survive and thrive.

Reconsider the eagle. To succeed, you must have faith in the process rather than act in fear like chickens do. This means eagles won't be found scratching around with the roosters and hens. Instead, he or she is filled with the ferocity of a conqueror and the determination to fly like an eagle.

"As an eagle that stirs up her nest that flutters over her young," it says in Deuteronomy 32:11. "He spread abroad His wings, and He took them, He bore them on His opinions." The eagle in this stanza is quite active; she agitates the nest, flutters over her young, stretches her wings wide, and carries them on her wings.

To reach new heights, you must grasp the full import of this verse and put your faith in the process rather than in the immediate results. I would like to explain the process of faith by using the illustration of an eagle's nest.

The eagle makes its nest high up on a rocky outcropping, with supporting ledges below and behind it. Tree limbs as large as two inches by six feet are used to construct the sturdy frame of the nest. When finished, an eagle's nest can be as deep as twenty feet and as wide as eight to ten feet.

When the female eagle lays the nest's foundation, she stops bringing home building materials and stays at the nest to complete the "finish work," but the male eagle keeps bringing home vines, leaves, animal hair, and whatever else he can find to finish the nest and "furnish" it.

The female lays two or three eggs once the nest is almost ready. She plucks feathers from her breast to line the nest for the eaglets before birth. She's the typical mother, eager to endure anything to ease her children's pain. The female eagle stays in bed and is fed by the male eagle while he tends to the eggs.

The male eagle keeps bringing home supplies for the nest. He might leave the nest for a while, only to come back with golf balls, tennis balls, old shoes, tin cans, and other glittering metal objects he finds. When the mother eagle decides the nest has become too cluttered, she will discard any unwanted items.

Meanwhile, eaglets begin to nibble at the shells of their eggs using a little, tooth-like appendage at the end of their beaks when the time comes for them to be born. Eaglets use this "tooth" to repeatedly peck at the shell until they break through.

God instills that kind of tenacity in eaglets from the start, so they can soar to great heights. It's important because it helps Eaglet develop coping mechanisms for when real-world challenges arise. In fact, I've heard that it's possible for an eaglet to perish if human attempts to help it hatch out of its egg. It needs a chance to be resilient and break free of its shell so it can live the way God intended. It must learn resilience so that it can keep going when things get tough. This is how God trains you when you journey through faith.

Eagle chicks don't leave their parents' carefully crafted nest for the first three months of their lives. It's substantial, roomy, strong, and warm. Mama is present, and life is wonderful. Their caretakers make their life simple and stress-free.

However, as the eaglets reach the age of twelve weeks, they experience a shocking development. Suddenly, their mother starts hurling all their playthings out of the window. She enters the nest and begins throwing everything out of there by beating on them with her wings.

The mother bird then proceeds to remove all the fluffy bedding from the nest, including the animal fur and feathers and replaces it with sharp sticks and thorns for the young to perch on. To explain this, consider the biblical allusion to the eagle mother who "stirs up her nest." She agitates the nest because she wants her young to leave it and learn to fly. They won't make it if she doesn't teach them how to fly.

Soon enough, the mother eagle starts taking charge. She starts gently prodding them to leave the nest. The young eaglets, unable to fly, plummet to the ground, perhaps in a state of extreme fear. They panic because they have no idea what is happening and do not want to look down at the rapidly coming ground. They hear the mother eagle swoop down and a whoosh as she catches them.

If a baby eagle could talk, I'm sure he'd say something like, "Oh! Praise the Lord! Oh, Mom, I was so frightened. You answered my question of whether or not you loved me by saving my life; therefore, obviously, you do.

Please take me back to the nest; I have no idea why you treated me that way. Please return my playthings. After returning the young to the nest, the mother eagle gently pushes them back out. Over and over, she goes through the same motions until they realize they must take to the air. The mother eagle sacrifices so much for her young because she loves them and wants them to have the best life possible. Most eaglets need this extra push to finally leave the nest. Unless you are also cornered, most times, you would rather stay in your familiar surroundings than face an unfamiliar situation and journey through faith.

Do you think God is taking care of you like a mother eagle does for her chicks? Has He recently taken away some of your playthings? Is He ripping away your nest's lining and leaving you to perch on thorny branches? Is He rearranging your life in ways that make you feel uneasy? Is He telling you to "Come on, it's time to fly"?

At times it can feel like God has abandoned you. You are in the dark about your life, and you fear that you will collapse to the ground at any moment, but when you are a faith walker, you resist the urge to give up under pressure when faced with something you don't know how to handle, you won't give in to fear.

Since God is a part of the journey, you must put your faith in Him, no matter what your eyes tell you. Never lose sight of the fact that the journey itself is of utmost importance if you want to succeed in the long run. Your eyes might be seeing the negativity, but trust the process because God is involved.

Trusting the process means that even if things may look bad in your current situation, it is not your destination. We must understand there is a timeframe between God's release and the manifestation. There is a gap in the middle called "The Process," which is also the waiting season that you must walk by faith, and it is in the middle where you're most vulnerable.

It's that process in the middle. If you're not careful, you will start listening to the enemy's voice and person's opinions.

It's the process in the middle where you start getting anxious, complaining, doubting, murmuring, cursing God, and walking out of God's will for your life.

I'm here to encourage you to Trust the process despite what you're seeing before your eyes. I have found out and personally experienced during this time of waiting in the process. God prepares us for His promise. It's during the process God teaches us, and our purpose comes forth.

It's the process in the middle; He develops and activates us, our strength, our character in him, our tenacity, our vitality, our faith, and our ability to soar.

It's the process in the middle our spiritual muscles and strengths are developed, the Fruits of the Spirits are being developed, and you're spiritually nourished.

It's in the process we're empowered to do exploits.

It's the process where our spiritual senses are activated.

During this time of waiting on God, He's pressing, pruning, sanctifying, processing, purifying, and preparing you for higher heights to maximize your potential.

Be encouraged when trusting the process to renew your mind, study the Word of God, Pray, Fast, Praise, and Worship, and build on a more meaningful, deeper relationship with Christ. Continue to stay humble in trusting the process because, in time, you will be exalted and soar.

You must remember as Children of God, there's "No Progress without Process!"

DAY 11

THE POWER OF A PRAYING PERSON

Eagle Christians need to spend time with God, but they also need to be selective about the outside influences they let in if they want to keep their vigor. With whom do you typically hang out? Who influences you and why? Where do you get your information?

A common assumption is that an eagle that frequently interacts with chickens will start to exhibit characteristics typical of chickens. To paraphrase *Proverbs 4:23: "Keep and guard your heart with all vigilance and above all that you guard, for out of it flow the springs of life."* Keep in mind that this expression is a command: "Guard your heart." You must protect your emotional safety. God will not keep your 777 safes. Be incredibly careful to protect your heart, for it is the source of everything that matters in life. In everyday terms, this means guarding your "ear gate" (your listening habits) and "the eye gate" (your visual intake) with extreme caution.

You need to be selective about the individuals you associate with; just as an eagle does not soar with all species of birds, you can't socialize with anybody and everyone. You become like the folks you hang out with the most. Conversely, if you put yourself in the company of upbeat people, you'll discover that your outlook shifts to match theirs. Spending time with misers will make you miserly while associating with givers will inspire you to raise the bar in your own giving.

To keep our strength soaring, we must be the type of people that seek out challenges from others. Here's some advice: ask God to surround you with people whose example will challenge you to raise the bar of your own behavior. God intends for you to improve yourself. It's important to continuously strive to improve your spiritual and personal development rather than resting on your laurels or settling for mediocrity.

God wants you to have the fortitude to weather any storm and carry out His intentions for your life. You need to strengthen your spiritual muscles for that to occur. You can't wish for spiritual strength; you have to work on developing it like you would develop a physical muscle. Praying is one of the methods of strengthening your spirituality and developing your muscles.

If you are willing to start doing what God is asking you to do, you will be astounded at how far you will go. God is always pushing you forward, so even if it isn't weightlifting, I'm sure He's dealing with you on something. Spiritual strength comes from doing the challenging things God asks.

Do not try to avoid the tough times since that is when you will find the power to soar. Things that were extremely challenging for you will become simple at some point. In truth, you soar like an eagle above the turmoil of life.

Praying stimulates your spiritual sense organ. Do you know that your natural senses of hearing and smell are as limited as your eyesight? Through prayer, your spiritual senses are activated, allowing you to see, hear, perceive, and know things that are not available to you in your normal state. The eagle's sense of sight is one of the most important to its ability to soar, so let's talk about it.

Eagles have two eyes, and their unique ability to see with both eyes are fascinating. The first set consists of their unaided eyesight. However, when they begin to soar on powerful wind thermals, a second eye begins to focus on them. They can use this backup sight to safely ride the powerful wind thermals while flying.

When they are spotted flying through real storm clouds, they employ their second eye, which is not the natural one, to help them navigate. The strong winds from a storm cloud may easily harm their normal, natural eye; thus, they rely on this second eye as a protective covering.

Christians also have two sets of eyes. The first pair consists of the eyes you are born with that help you to observe your physical environment. You also have the second eyes, the eyes of the Spirit, which help you see things from God's perspective. Since all Christians have the Holy Spirit dwelling inside us, you also have access to His eyes so that you can see things as He does at various times.

Prayer fuels your personal relationship with the Lord and will develop to the point where He will let you "see" things from His perspective. You will begin to "get" many Bible passages, possible interpretations and revelations. You will begin to "see" the truth about many issues in your own life.

When this begins to happen, it is because the Holy Spirit is opening your eyes to see the world as He does. When this starts happening, it will be extremely supernatural. It's God giving you a glimpse of eternity's past, present, and future.

According to the Bible, you'll be free if you know the truth. However, you must become aware of the nature of that reality before it may begin to liberate you.

You need both our physical eyes and the spiritual eyes of the Holy Spirit working in you so that you might do God's job effectively in this world, just as the eagle requires both of his eyes to fly and hunt. This is the power of prayer; it opens you up to spiritual realities and the spiritual realm. You cannot soar without your eyes, both physical and spiritual.

DAY 12
ONE WORD FROM GOD CAN CHANGE EVERYTHING IN YOUR LIFE

(Hebrews 4:12), "For the word of God is full of living power. It is sharper than the sharpest knife, cutting deep into our innermost thoughts and desires. It exposes us for what we really are."

God's Word has the power to renew, refresh, and revive. A word from God is the foundation upon which you build every success and breakthrough.

(Isaiah 55:10-11), assures us that God's Word is always effective; it does whatever it has been sent to do. This is the word that you need, the word that never fails. Remember that creation begins to take shape only after God speaks. When He spoke, form and order appeared where only chaos and disorder existed.

Do you feel like there is nothing to your life? God's Word is all you need to be changed and given form. If you feel helpless and aimless, He can give you strength and purpose with just a word. Though there will be times when you find it hard to believe what God says, this is the truth, but it does stop the potency of God's Word. God's Word is capable of completely altering your future.

Will you submit to His Word and let it transform you? Will you clear out enough mental room to take His word to heart? Or will the noise of today's routine, work, and worries drown it out?

If you would own it, receive it, create a place for it, understand it, meditate on it, yield to it, and seize it, the Word of God has the potential to transform your life and the lives of others around you. God's Word can reveal your true motives and thoughts *(Hebrews 4:12)*. Soul and spirit are torn apart in a profound way. It connects your negative compulsive behavior with the reality of God's Word in your heart and mind.

It is quite unfortunate that many Christians don't know and experience the potency of God's Word because they just hear the word, don't meditate, and don't put it into practice. Apostle James advises strongly in *(James 1:22), "But be doers of the word, and not only hearers of it, blinding yourselves with false ideas."*

Unfortunately, there are many who pray, and after praying, they still experience increased anxiety and worry afterward. You have memorized His Word, yet you hardly ever put it into practice. You cannot be transformed and revived by just memorizing His word. The potency of His word is in your obedient to it.

How do you let His truth possess, motivate, and propel you to the point where you become a living testimony empowered by the Holy Spirit to advance Christ's kingdom? You can only encounter God in His Word. Below are some steps to take to make God's word effective in your life.

1. Spend time in solitude praying for an experience with God. When you meet God, you will never be the same. The turning point in Jacob's life came after a solitary encounter with God.

2. Meditate on and cling to the Word of God, which is able to transform you.

3. Make it a practice to prioritize God each day.

4. Use the knowledge you find in the Bible as the Spirit's Sword to destroy evil.

5. Act righteously and rely on God's word.

Hearing one word from God can change your entire posture.

Hearing one word from God can change your situation.

Hearing one word from God can change your entire life.

Hearing one word from God can change your mindset.

Hearing one word from God can change your focus.

Hearing one word from God can change your lifestyle.

Hearing one word from God can give you hope.

Hearing one word from God can give you peace.

Hearing one word from God can give you breakthroughs.

Hearing one word from God can give you deliverance.

Hearing one word from God can give you freedom.

Hearing one word from God can give you love.

Hearing one word from God can give you encouragement.

But the question I would like to ask you is, are you in the right position to receive the word from God? So that the word from God can change your life and your present circumstances!

For that Word to manifest and be activated into your life, you must be correctly positioned and aligned to receive it; you must be in the right frame of mind so that when the Word of God is released, it will propel you from your situation to destiny. You need that one word from God that will bring transformation through Jesus Christ.

DAY 13

THE POWER OF AN INTIMATE
RELATIONSHIP WITH CHRIST

Relationships with Christ range widely from one individual to the other. Becoming a believer of Christ, or "being converted," does not automatically imply a close personal relationship with Christ.

There are people who believe that prayer and weekly church attendance are the only necessary steps to have a meaningful relationship with Christ. They accept Christ as a sacrifice for their sins but have no further connection with Him. Others look to Christ as a model for how they live their lives. However, they don't really anticipate having much of a relationship with Him because He is in Heaven, and they are on Earth. The best word to describe such connections to Christ is "distant."

Going to church on the same day each week is completely different from developing a personal relationship with Christ. Being a worshipper on Sunday morning and being a Christian are two different things. Plenty of individuals in the world like that don't show any fruit either; they are not Christians. Sitting in a church pew doesn't transform you into a Christian, the way sitting in the garage does not turn you into a car. Jesus died to facilitate a personal relationship with God, not a religion. That connection with God, through Christ, will fortify you, assist you in navigating life, and transform your experience from "frustration" to "victory."

To this effect, the Bible teaches that followers of Christ can have a living, breathing connection with the Lord. After all, He is a living, breathing human being, not some abstract "theological concept" who once walked the planet but is now very far away. He overcomes sin and death while experiencing the same temptations you do. *(Romans 6:8; Hebrews 4:15)* He is loyal, and as such, He has all the power and grace you need to conquer sin in your life. This also means that your relationship with Him can be vibrant and dynamic rather than flat and unchanging, as He is a living being. *(Revelation 1:18).*

The truth is that only you can choose the kind of faith in Christ you want to have. To have a personal relationship with Christ, you must first make the decision to believe that such a relationship is possible; in the spiritual realm, everything is the result of a person's faith.

Following Christ is not one-sided. It is made apparent by Jesus' words in *(John 14:23)*, *"If anyone loves Me, he will keep My word; and My Father will love him, and We will come to him and make Our home with him."* Imagine that God the Father and Jesus Christ are interested in making your life their home! Is that how you and Christ relate to one another?

And again, the Lord declares in *(John 14:21)*, *"Those who obey my commandments are the ones who love me. And because they love me, my Father will love them, and I will love them. And I will reveal myself to each one of them."* Do you believe Christ wants to make Himself known to you? It's obvious that such a revelation of Christ is to occur throughout your life as a Christian, not just at the beginning of your Christian life, because that promise is given to those who love Him and fulfill His commandments.

Intimate Relationship with Christ

If you choose to meet these requirements (of having an intimate relationship with Christ), Christ will become a dear friend with whom you can enjoy constant communion. Through the power of the Holy Spirit, He will not be distant but rather always present in your innermost thoughts and feelings. Is it not true that He told us, "The kingdom of heaven is within you?" Your relationship with the One you claim to worship will be one of constant discourse. He's not only a friend who won't leave you when times become tough but also someone who knows what it's like to struggle with temptation. When facing adversity, you can draw strength from His words of wisdom and support. He rescues you from the punishment you deserve, and the control sin exerts over your life. According to the psalmist in *(Psalm 46:1), He is "...a very present help in time of need,"* This is the power of having an intimate relationship with Christ. He was fully human when He came to redeem man, so He can empathize with you when you are vulnerable. *(Hebrews 4:15).*

Your faith in Christ is a spiritual, mental, and emotional reality. When your love is focused on Him, He takes His rightful place as King in your life. Whenever a new idea strikes you, ask yourself sincerely, "Dear Lord Jesus, is this thought pleasing in Your sight?" Such an outlook helps your heart grasp the nature of the mind of Christ, which is the mind of the Spirit, the nature of life and peace. You discover that some mental processes fill you with vitality and calm while others leave you feeling empty and unfulfilled. This is how you develop the ability to tell the difference between what is good and what is bad, between what is pleasing to God and what is not. You can learn how to live a more Spirit-filled life through an intimate relationship with Christ.

Your relationship with Christ extends to your human spirit, where you learn to look aside from your own ideas and feelings and instead to Him in times of stress, hardship, and temptation. Christ's Spirit, who is the spirit of prophecy, is waiting to meet you there. *(Revelation 19:10).* You will feel a tremendous upsurge in strength as the prophetic spirit of Christ offers words of edification, exhortation, and comfort directly to your human spirit.

The words of the Bible that you have read, heard, and spoken many times before will come to life for you as you get closer to Christ. Once dry and meaningless, verses will be bursting with the strength to live as Christ did. You will feel a spirit of revelation speaking to your conscience, which will change how you interpret the Bible and your life. Your faith will be nourished and grow with each new understanding of God's Word. And the Spirit's influence in your life will increase as your faith does, empowering you to walk more closely in Christ's footsteps.

A More Intimate Union with Christ

Human connections are dynamic in the sense that they evolve and deepen through time. The same holds true for your relationship with Christ. Your walk with Christ can be like a fresh start every day, just like God's mercies. As your affection for Him grows and your preference for your own fades, your relationship grows stronger.

(Revelation 3:20), "Look! Here I stand at the door and knock. If you hear me calling and open the door, I will come in, and we will share a meal as friends."

According to this above Bible verse, Christ says 'you.' Are you that person?

Maybe you have been a Christian for a long time, but you have never had a chance to get to know Christ on a personal level. He is trying to get your attention today; can you hear His voice? Do not merely accept Him as a sacrifice for your sins, but welcome Him into your heart as a dear and valued Friend, as Lord and Master, as one whom you desire to rule and reign in your heart and life.

If you take Christ at His word, welcome Him as Lord and Master into your life. Do this, and you will know the joy and peace that comes with having an intimate relationship with Christ. The King of kings and Lord of lords will get personally involved in your life.

DAY 14

BREAKING DOWN THE PROTOCOL OF MEN AND STANDING ON THE PROTOCOL OF CHRIST

The best way to rise through the ranks of any government, organization, or church is to follow the established protocols and norms that have been established over time. Even inside households, a set of customs and norms must be followed.

For example, I can't just get in my car and go to the White House whenever I want to see the President of the United States. There is a protocol for requesting an audience with the President. It's possible that I will need to meet with his assistant or send him a formal letter before I can speak with him. This is a proper use of a protocol. Following established norms and procedures can help keep things running smoothly. Even God respects protocols. His actions are methodical. He has His own method for accomplishing tasks and influencing people to give them to Him.

What exactly is a protocol? It's the formal process by which a state manages its affairs, a group's norms, or a formal agreement or treaty.

The protocols of men are the norms of the modern world for getting ahead and accomplishing great things. You can't soar to greater heights when you operate on the protocol of men or the norms of men; instead, you must shatter those protocols and build your life on Christ's. *In (Romans 12:1-2), the apostle Paul writes, "Do not be conformed by this world; rather, be changed from the inside out by a new way of thinking. Then you will know what is acceptable and pleasant to God and what is perfect, and you will be able to choose accordingly."* The will of God is for all His children to soar high as the eagle, but not standing on the protocol of Christ will make your soaring impossible.

Christ's standard and operating procedure necessitates a mental reset before any soaring is even feasible. As infants, we all adopt practices, ideas, and attitudes that run counter to Christ's teachings; this is why you must have your mind renewed first. Flying high isn't easy or achievable when based on men's protocol, but it is possible when based on Christ's procedure, which is based on holiness and righteousness.

What, then, does Christ's protocol entail? *(2 Timothy 2:19), "Nevertheless the foundation of God stands sure, having this seal, The Lord knows them that are His. And, let everyone that names the name of Christ depart from iniquity."*

Christ's standards of conduct disapprove of sin, immorality, expediency, and dishonesty. Stay away from evil deeds if you wish to be lifted higher by the Holy Spirit. Soaring will be a mirage if the proper procedure of purity and righteousness is not in place.

I get that you want to break through the ceiling, but are you holy in your aspirations? Do you try to keep your life clean? Are you in the right standing with God? If the answer is no, then you need to make amends with God and get in line with Him before He can lift you up.

You will never see God, have a relationship with Him, or submit to His mandate while you are living in everlasting sin; thus, you will never be able to break the protocol of men. The ability to soar is diminished by sin and wrongdoing.

DAY 15
IT'S JUST A TEST! DON'T QUIT!

You probably know some folks who have had miraculous interventions from God. I know you will enjoy hearing the inspiring stories of people's lives, but you must know that there is adversity behind every remarkable story. A test always precedes testimony. There are many challenges in life but overcoming them is essential to reaching your full potential and soaring on eagle's wings.

Understanding the significance of hardship in your life is crucial for surviving it and emerging stronger on the other side. Whatever God allows you to go through is for your ultimate good, no matter how bad it hurts, how unfair it is, or how terrible it is. If you accept adversity and don't try to escape it, you can gain valuable lessons that will make you better people in the long term.

In the same way that tests "try" you, trials "try" you as well. Most of the time, they are meant to serve as character-building mirrors. Until you are put to the test, you will never know if the positive things you believe about yourself are indeed true. When you are put to the test, the true nature of your generosity, honesty, or commitment to the truth or ideal becomes apparent, no matter how much you like to think otherwise. Test reveals the true you.

Until your convictions are put to the test, you will never know what you genuinely believe. A person's level of godliness is revealed only when their faith is being tested. You can't know how you will react until the pressure is extremely high. Until you have to be polite to someone when you don't want to, you have no idea if you have a good heart.

When you are tested, your character and dedication are shown for what they are. Tests are beneficial because they confirm the good qualities you already possess and highlight the areas where you may improve. Accept your flaws without shame. The power of God is designed to help you in your areas of weakness.

Why did Jesus, God in the flesh, have to go through the ordeal of being tempted by the devil in the wilderness after the forty days and forty nights of fasting? God the Father had no reason to think Jesus would give in to temptation. I believe Jesus, in His humanity, went into the wilderness to strengthen His resolve and prove to the devil that He would remain loyal to His heavenly Father no matter what.

You can't expect others to be fighting your battles for you, always praying for you and facing your giants. You can't keep depending on your Pastor or your leader. Leaders and others can only pray for you so much, but eventually, you will have to learn how to pray for yourself. You must acquire the skill of independently locating sacred texts and the secret place of God. You need to acquire the skill of assertiveness to fight and overcome all.

You need to put God first in your life to the point where He is your primary resource whenever you encounter difficulty. Instead of turning to your pastor, friends, or others for guidance, you should look to Him, the Author, and the Finisher of your Faith. Peter tells us in *(1 Peter 4:12)* that your test and trials are for your benefit: *"Dear friends, don't be surprised at the fiery trials you are going through, as if something strange were happening to you."*

One reason you must go through tests is to see how well you perform. Sometimes, you wish you had the faith of Sister XYZ. Have you ever given it a thought that, for her to have had a robust faith, it was not something she stumbled upon? Strong faith is developed like strong muscles in the fires or midst of adversity.

Those who have accomplished great things for God have never had it easy. If you want to accomplish great things for God, you need to develop character, and the only way to do that is to persevere through the challenges of life while remaining true to God through Jesus Christ.

James states in *(James 1:2-3), "Consider it fully pleasant, my brethren, whenever you are immersed in or meet difficulties of any sort or fall into numerous temptations. Have faith and know that the testing of your faith will produce in you perseverance, steadfastness, and patience."*

Before your trials teach you perseverance and patience, they will reveal many other flaws in your character, perspectives, and ways of thinking. God permits you to go through adversity to reveal your true character. Nothing can be done until you can expose them. Once you recognize them, you will begin taking steps toward overcoming them with God's aid.

God does not permit adversity because He takes pleasure in your pain but rather so that you may come to understand your total dependence on Him. Truth is what sets you free, so you should never be afraid of it *(John 8:32)*.

According to *(James 1:3)*, everything you go through helps you in the long run because it makes you stronger and builds your endurance, develops godly character, helps you to know yourself, and allows you to deal with things on an honest level with God and take care of them so you can move on.

Make up your mind that the next time you are put to the test, you will see that it is for your own good. Tell God, "All right, Lord, I think this will turn out great for me; I know that you will ultimately work this out for my benefit." If you give God your trust, He can make a way out of no way!

THE WORK FOR YOUR TRIALS

Eagle parents often raise their young far from human civilization in a remote nest they construct for their young. This is done to ensure that she can bring children up in a secure environment free from harm.

Similarly, the Lord occasionally uses adversity to strengthen His eagles. Again, Moses spent 40 years in the desert's secluded backside before God brought him out to execute history's greatest deliverance.

David probably spent 13 to 15 years hiding in the desert caves before God summoned him to become Israel's greatest king.

Some of you may be currently experiencing the Lord's gradual elevation in your call to service in the desert. Your greatest spiritual growth in Him will come at moments like these when you are in a situation reminiscent of the wilderness.

When you're in the midst of adversity, many are facing challenging times, and trying times, but I'm here to tell you It's a Test! Don't Quit!

DAY 16

NOTHING IS IMPOSSIBLE WITH GOD

Have you ever been in such a dire strait that you had no choice but to cry out to God? In situations like this, the best things to do are pray, worship, read the Word, and spend time in the presence of God when it seems there is no way out. When you pray, worship, and read the Bible, you are taking your mind off the situation and turning to the one who is not bound by the same constraints you are. Who is all-powerful, all-knowing, the I am that I am. You put your faith in the God who can do any and everything.

The world around us is one that is doomed to disaster. Wars, famines, and bad people may be found just about anywhere. The issues of this world including basic human necessities like trust, peace, abundance, and righteous leaders are even harder to come by. Unless God intervenes, our world will continue down its current disastrous path, and this brings about impossibility to the world. God's intervention in history to save His people begins with the birth of His only begotten son Jesus Christ. This is God; this is how He operates; anytime He wants to do the impossible, He will start an insignificant event to prove that He is the God of all possibility.

This is how most of God's creations begin. He often begins with a tiny step when God plans a massive undertaking. He always begins with the impossible when attempting a miracle. Remember, God didn't send Jesus to Jerusalem, Paris, or London when he sent his Son into the world. He dispatched him to a town in Israel known as Bethlehem. In order to demonstrate his will, God enjoys taking humble beginnings. Let us look at some acts of the God of possibilities.

He imagines the unimaginable and makes it happen. That, of course, sums up Abraham's entire existence. God discovered this heathen in the Ur of the Chaldeans. He is 75 and a bachelor with no offspring. God assured the elderly man that his offspring would number as numerous as the sand on the beach and the stars in the sky. There are too many of them for anyone to count.

It's incredible that God uses questions to change minds and clarify his intervention. Something supernatural is about to take place when the IMMORTAL God begins questioning human beings. It's clear that the All-Powerful God is preparing to accomplish something beyond the ken of mere mortals when He begins to query their meager abilities with rhetorical inquiries. Typically, God will pose a question to a man that only He, as the All-Powerful God, can truly answer. Despite our inquisitive nature, God provides us with the right solution to every problem we have ever encountered.

God once questioned Ezekiel, *"Will the dry bones live again?"* *(Ezekiel 37:3)* Then He asked me, "Son of man, can these bones live?" And I said, "Thou knowest, O Lord God." Ezekiel's response to God was the epitome of tact and diplomacy.

He reverted to control of the situation back to God. His response was, *"LORD, Thou knowest. "The question was also posed to SARAH by God. (Genesis 18:14) Is There Anything the Lord Can't Do?* I will come back to you at the proper time in your life, and Sarah will give birth to a son. Sarah had been in clinical and severe menopause for over 40 years, and it was evident that she was facing an age-long barrenness. It seemed improbable that a woman of 90 could conceive and give birth to a child. But God visited Sarah as she inquired whether the issue was too challenging for God to rectify. Sarah finally got pregnant and had Isaac. Verse 11 of Hebrews 11 says even Sarah, who was barren and too old to have children, was able to conceive through faith. She had faith that God would fulfill His word.

During their time in the desert, the Israelites relied on Moses to provide them with protein. Moses told God that there weren't enough wild animals to go around. *(Numbers 11:21-22)*, And Moses answered the Lord, saying,

"Shall the flocks and the herds be slain for them, to satiate them? For the people, among whom I am, are six hundred thousand footmen; and thou hast said, I will give them flesh, that they may eat a whole month. Or shall all the fish in the sea be gathered up for them to satisfy their hunger?"

In *(Numbers 11:23)*, however, God questioned Moses in response. "Is the Lord's Hand Too Short to Save You? the LORD asked Moses. Now you will discover if what I have said about you will happen." God provided nutrition for the Israelites for forty years as they wandered in the desert.

On one occasion, when Jesus needed to feed a large crowd in a desert area, JESUS asked his disciples, "Where can we buy bread?". According to the Bible, Jesus had the answers while his disciples were puzzled over economic and financial matters. In the middle of the desert, JESUS lavishly fed the crowd with 5 loaves and 2 fishes that He blessed and miraculously multiplied.

(John 6:12-13) When everyone had eaten their fill, Jesus instructed His followers to collect the leftovers so that nothing would go to waste. They did so, and the remnants of the five barley loaves filled twelve baskets.

Is there anything in your life that is too difficult for the Lord to handle today? The problems, challenges, impossibilities, equations, questions, etc., in your life are going to vanish because God is about to do something about it. God is about to step into your situation.

The Bible promises that if you put your faith in God, He will make a way where there seems to be none. The Bible says, *"If you can believe, then all things are possible to him that believeth"* (Mark 9:23). As soon as you put your faith in God, God's power will be unleashed mightily on your behalf. The Bible says that God's power is extremely great for anyone who puts their faith in Him. *(Ephesians 1:19) says, "And what is the exceeding Greatness of His Power toward those who believe, according to the working of His Mighty Power."* Tell your heavenly Father God that you are giving Him everything that is impossible for you to handle today. *(Mark 10:27) And Jesus, gazing at them, said, "With men this is impossible, but not with God; for with God all things are possible."*

God is about to make all your impossible situations possible; give it to Him. He's in control!

DAY 17

THE POWER LIES IN YOU TO OVERCOME THE STORM

Everyone faces storms at certain times in life. Storms of situations, circumstances, difficulties, obstacles, and sometimes problems. Storms of life come to take us off course, distract us from the path God designs us to follow and be who He had created us to be. Have you ever noticed that when the storm is on the horizon, eagles don't do what other birds do; they head straight for it? When it starts to rain, an eagle won't leave its nest until it's soaked through. The eagle is powerless to halt the storm, yet it can soar above its destructive path. When an eagle detects a storm on the horizon, it will wait for the thermal current of the storm to carry it to a higher altitude, where it may then soar above the storm rather than through it.

Chickens are always afraid of storms; they dare not face storms. When you study chickens, you will notice that they are often timid, fearful of life, lethargic, and don't live up to their full potential. Farmyards are just places for chickens to scratch the ground and crow. Chickens flap their wings, yet they do not actually fly high to the point of soaring. They are content with their fenced-in existence because of the necessity of doing so. They are too fragile for the outside world and need to be confined to a chicken yard. You will notice that when a storm rolls in, the chickens' first instinct is to flap around in the chicken yard, stirring up dirt, and then to run into the chicken coop, where they will huddle together in terror while hoping to discover a grub worm.

As the characteristics of a chicken are described, many Christians operate like a chicken. Whenever the storm of life arises and troubles happen, they "flap around" and "run for the chicken coop." They are not living the victorious life that Jesus Christ died to give. You cannot avoid facing life's inevitable storms by constantly seeking shelter. According to *(Romans 8:37)*, you have already won the war. Because God is with you, even in the midst of trouble, you can rest easy. God has called you to be overcomers, not victims of fear and intimidation. So, the power to overcome any storm that comes your way is in you. The power to live victoriously is what Christ has given you, don't be a chicken that becomes timid in the face of the storm. In the storm, our greatest potential is being maximized and developed.

When clouds form, eagles get excited because they know a storm is on the way. Once the eagles have located the storm's wind, they use it to soar above the clouds. The eagle may soar and relax its wings while the other birds are busy hiding in the tree's branches and foliage. Goal-getters, on the other hand, welcome and profit from difficulties. Who are you, an eagle or a chicken?

Without proper forethought and planning, you won't be able to weather the storms.

Every morning, an eagle starts there day by sitting on a rock and individually putting all his wing feathers (there can be as many as 1,200 on each wing) into his mouth. He has a specialized oil gland near his tail and exhales that oil onto each feather. This process, known as "preening," is analogous to steam cleaning and takes about an hour. It restores the eagle's feathers to pristine condition, seals out moisture, and gets them ready for the day's soaring. The eagle's survival and performance at his best depend on him making these preparations.

Not many Christians find the time to be their best every day; therefore, they never find the strength to soar. How can you be your best every day? It is by spending time in the presence of God. Time spent with God each day is the finest way to ensure optimal strength throughout the day. Taking time to pray, read the Bible, worship, and meditate in the morning will do more to prepare you for the challenges ahead of you.

All I can say is that the more you have on your plate and the busier you are, the more time you need to devote to God. The time you give to God is more valuable than the time you give to your career, work, and social media, but I don't know how your schedule needs to change to accommodate God first. The more time you give Him, the more time He will return to you. He controls time, so He can safeguard it and teach you how to best use it to get what you really need to be done.

Choose to devote time to Him. Give up trying to squeeze God into your busy life and instead make Him your first priority. The more time you give Him, the more time He will return to you. He controls the flow of time. He is the existence of time.

You don't have to go through life afraid! You don't have to let your heart be troubled! You don't have to face the storm of life alone! In *(St. John 14: 27)*, *"Peace I leave with you.; my peace I give you. I do not give you as the world gives. Do not let your heart be troubled, and do not be afraid."* If you allow fear to take you over during the storm of life, you won't be able to make it or survive another day. The most important thing you can do for yourself if you're going through the storm right now, is give it to God, put your faith in Him, and trust Him. I guarantee you that He will comfort you, reassure you, and keep you safe through it all because He cares for you. The best thing you can do for yourself is to develop those eagle characteristics and face the storm with courage, stability, prayer, worship, and meditation. The more time you spend in His presence, the more power you will receive to overcome the storm of life. Paul said in *(Philippians 4: 13) "I can do all things through Christ who strengthens me."*

The power lies in you to rise above all your storm like an eagle. Storms don't dictate your life, but what dominates you is what God has done in you and through you. As a Child of God, to overcome any storms of life, first, you need to know who you are in Christ and to know that the power lies in you through. You also need to know what Jesus Christ has done for you on the Calvary cross, in the resurrection, and the sending of The Holy Spirit, and to know that He's sitting at the right hand of our father making intercession for you.

You can avoid being blindsided by life and allowing it to take you by surprise. Spend time with God daily to prepare yourself for the storms that may arise, so you can have the spiritual fortitude to soar on wings like the eagles.

DAY 18
STOP BLAMING OTHERS

Does placing blame on other people help you get over your problem? Does blaming others make your situation better? No way, no how! So instead of wasting time assigning blame, take stock of the position of your heart.

You may be unfamiliar with the concept of "victimism." This is the result of placing blame on others for your difficulties. It is an attempt to make sense of why things haven't gone according to plan. You have gotten the raw end of the deal and had bad luck with the cards life threw you. Is this how you view life? Then the victim label fits you. That's how you make it through life: by placing the blame for everything that goes wrong on everyone else.

It's likely to get a bad grade at work if you submit a report late. Take accountability instead of blaming others, and say something like, "I would have turned it in earlier, but Frank was late getting the statistics to me."

If you have had some experience being a victim, you will know that for a long time, the victim's rallying cry will be, "It's not my fault." It is not always clear whose fault it is, but you can always be sure it is not your own. If it isn't your fault, it must be perhaps your parents. Nowadays, people tend to attribute all forms of mental disease to them. If it isn't one of your parents, it's probably one of your siblings.

You will begin to think it was because you were always mistreated or they constantly ignored you. There are plenty of other potential candidates in the world that you might blame apart from your parent. Perhaps it was your forebears who tainted you. Maybe it was the high school gang you hanged with. Perhaps you got mixed up with the wrong crowd and became corrupted by them, or perhaps you hung around with the wrong set of people and became morally superior to yourself. You may always place the blame on your husband. After all, he is most likely a melon-headed fool. Your wife is to be blamed she definitely has her flaws. It could also be the co-workers. Exactly what I was looking for! They are nothing but a dishonest, treacherous lot. And it keeps going. This is a bad attitude for anyone who will soar on an eagle's wings.

There is logic to every human proficiency at assigning blame. Explanations are in our blood; it's just what we do naturally; it's like the lifeblood of our souls. Passing the buck is a time-honored human practice.

Back in the Garden of Eden *(Genesis 3)*, let's rewind a bit. Let's zero in on the time immediately following Adam and Eve's ingestion of the infamous apple. To the uninitiated, it is still a paradise. Adam's face breaks into a goofy, guilty grin as he digests the fruit. He's done wrong but has no idea what consequences will follow.

So much occurs so rapidly. Something about Eve that he hasn't seen before catches his eye. She is completely naked. That took him by surprise. Then he lowers his head and realized he is also barefoot. At that moment, the thought occurs to him, "We better cover up ourselves."

But where did you get that idea? It was the product of a mind that had just experienced sin for the first time. Because Adam and Eve had no concept of their own nakedness, they had never worn clothing. The first effect of falling is being exposed to public shame.

Guilt follows on the heels of sin and the guilt of being exposed is far worse. Then there were some eerie footfalls to follow. It's the Lord strolling around the garden on a sunny afternoon.

Adam and Eve instinctively (and I use that word deliberately) cover their tracks. Why? Who ordered them into hiding? They didn't need any explanation from anyone. Their own guilty hearts convicted them. The consequences of disobedience are starting to show. Once in close communion with God, sin has severed their connection to their Maker. The second effect of the fall is that people begin to run from God.

But the time has come for the truth to be revealed. Adam responds to God's call, "I heard you in the garden, and I was afraid because I was naked, so I hid." Once sin entered the scene, Adam no longer felt comfortable standing before God without covering up.

Then comes the follow-up query: "Have you eaten from the tree that I commanded you not to eat of?" Adam blamed Eve, saying, "The woman that you put here with me, she gave me some fruit from the tree, and I ate it."

Adam shifted the blame to cover up for his own guilt. But that's not the end of the story yet. A puzzled God looks at Eve and says, "What is this you have done?" She also shifted the blame by saying: "The serpent deceived me, and I ate."

What makes those two options so difficult to choose between? Technically, Adam and Eve were both telling the truth. When Adam said that Eve gave him the fruit, he wasn't lying. When Eve said the serpent tricked her, she wasn't lying. But they were both inventing justifications for absolving themselves of blame. When Adam had Eve to blame, he didn't have to take the blame for anything. As long as the serpent was to be blamed, Eve would appear to be a helpless victim.

The Effect of Placing Blame on Others

The story above clarifies a lot of questions. First, it reveals that placing blame on others is intrinsic to the human condition. Second, it shows that when you are free to make your own decisions, you will find excuses to shirk responsibility. Third, it reveals that shifting blame to others is usually just a way of subtly distorting the truth to absolve your own responsibility. Fourth, it informs you that you are doomed to repeat Adam and Eve's sin until the mercy of God is deeply worked inside you.

Our culture encourages you to look outside of yourself for the causes of your difficulties, and you go along with it because assigning blame is a part of your religious DNA. It's in your fallen human nature to shift blame to someone else. The first buck passer was Adam, and the second was Eve. They weren't the final ones, though. So many have come a long way in a thousand years.

The End of Adam

The good news of Jesus Christ becomes especially important in this context. The word "gospel" is derived from the Greek for "good news." Jesus Christ offers hope for true and enduring transformation, especially in areas where patterns, routines, and traditions have been established since Adam. To put it another way, Paul was telling us that just as *"in Adam all die, so in Christ, all will be made alive." (1 Corinthians 15:22)*. That scripture is typically associated with the day of the resurrection. However, the same is true for the present. The legacy of Adam is one of suffering, frustration, and ultimately death. When Adam sinned, he gave us our first taste of guilt and humiliation. He taught us how to evade God's wrath. He instructed us in the art of shifting blame to avoid taking any blame for our actions. That's the legacy that Adam left us.

However, *"grace superabundance" occurred "where sin abounded." (Romans 5:20)* You believe in Jesus Christ; He has resurrected you from the grave. The time has come to finally put an end to your Adamic ways. It is possible to break the habit of apologizing for everything. Putting the blame on others for your difficulties is a habit that must be broken if you will soar higher.

Are You Seeking Restoration? Do you want to be free from this awful habit? There is one important thing that you must do. You must realize how much help you need and desire to be changed by Jesus Christ. That is all you need and nothing less.

As I conclude this section, let me buttress the above point with a story in the Bible.

John 5 contains a beautiful narrative that highlights this problem. Jesus had visited Jerusalem for one of the annual festivals. Hundreds of thousands of Israelis came to make the pilgrimage. One of the places he went to while there was Bethesda, also known as "the house of mercy." It was a pool in the northeastern part of the city, close to the Sheep Gate. The pool area features five colonnades (or porches). One author described it as the "Jewish Lourdes" of its day. At regular intervals, an angel, in Jewish belief, would come and stir the waters. After the water has been churned, whoever gets in first will be cured of their illnesses.

Hundreds of individuals who were obviously ill or disabled congregated around the pool, expecting that the water would be agitated. Jesus encountered a man who had been sick for 38 years on the day He passed by. After learning the man's paralysis had persisted for so long, He asked, "Do you want to be well?"

It's a strange query at first thought. The man's presence begs the question: why? Naturally, he desired good health. Did Jesus think he was stupid? Absolutely not! His inquiry was of the utmost gravity. Because it was possible that the man did not want to become better, he was curious.

Do I want to be healed?" the man asks. What a bizarre inquiry. Can you explain why I am here? Obviously, you're a newcomer. The issue is lost on you. Someone always seems to get there before me whenever the angel comes to stir the water. Eventually, no one will come to my aid. They simply move aside for me. Is there a sadder tale than this one? Isn't that sad? He kept blaming people for not carrying him into the water and remained there for 38 years. What a tragedy!

Jesus told the man, Stop making other people responsible for your distress. I can heal you. However, I will not use my authority until you express a desire to recover. If I make you well, you won't have time to sit around and chit-chat. If I cure you, you won't need to beg any longer. If I cure you, you won't be able to use your condition as an excuse for preferential treatment at home. If I heal you, you won't need as much pity. Being healthy doesn't come cheap. Do you Want to make the payment?" Jesus asked the man, "Do you really want to be changed?" If you desire a change, then anything is possible. If the question is answered with a negative, not even Jesus can save the man, and this also applies to you; if you don't desire to be changed by Jesus Christ, He cannot force Himself on you.

I don't mean to scare you, but rather, to be honest. The divine Son of God exemplifies the ideal of a gentleman. If you don't let Him in, He won't bother you. It is up to you to decide whether or not you wish to be altered by Him.

It's possible you felt like a failure for a very long time. It always seems like a four-touchdown loss when you add up the final score.

This is the good news: If you put your faith in Christ, you have already won. Grace is all about doing things like this. He can turn perennial losers into everlasting champions. He takes those who have given up and offers them a reason to believe in a better tomorrow. Those who are unfortunate find themselves on the receiving end of his royal grace.

You might be reading this right now and probably feel like an utter loser. You have put in a lot of effort, yet it seems like the more you try, the further behind you get. It's accurate to a certain extent. The mud and filth of defeat after defeat had caked on your face.

Do you find yourself wanting to place blame on those around you? Do you feel like taking the mud and slop and dumping it on them? Do not take such an action! They will get dirtier from you doing this and attempts to purify yourself will fail. Throwing dirt at another person won't make it go away.

The Divine Gardener will step in and tend to your soul if you're ready to take charge of your life. He has the power to make amends for your shortcomings. The mud and slime are no match for his composting skills, and new life can spring up from the muck of your defeat.

That's something He's capable of doing. Grace is all about doing things like this. But you must refrain from becoming a jerk and dumping that on other people. At some point, you just need to claim some ground as your own. The process of restoration starts with that action. Something lovely will emerge from the soil of your terrible mistakes after the Divine Gardener has finished His work.

DAY 19

IGNORE THE NEGATIVES

Do you know there have been and will always be gloomy individuals? Neither you nor I can do anything to alter that fact. But we can learn to tune out the distractions. You can keep moving toward your goals by learning to ignore the naysayers.

If you have ever tried to accomplish something in your life but kept running into roadblocks and skepticism from others, know that you are not alone. There will always be naysayers who insist that you can't achieve your goals because you lack requisite qualities (e.g., intelligence, money, connections, skills, etc.). But if you want to succeed, you must tune out the naysayers.

Positive energy can be stifled by negative force. It's amazing how effectively destructive negative thoughts, comments, and actions can be.

It only takes one disparaging word to start a rumor, leading to a false witness and an awful situation. The spread of bad vibes occurs when one individual interacts with another. Everyone has encountered a pessimist. They are everywhere: our children, teachers, co-workers, neighbors, in-laws, and, yes, fellow churchgoers. There are some who complain; they are rarely content. Some people are cruel and angry, and rude. Others, meanwhile, are bitter, spiteful, caustic, egotistical, and unapproachable. It's common sense for you to keep your distance.

Others, however, care solely about themselves and would stop at nothing to achieve their ends, regardless of the damage they cause in the process. For some of us, fending off the barrage of criticism is an ongoing struggle. The spirit takes a serious beating from life's setbacks. Unchecked, we risk becoming the same gloomy, unhappy people we condemn and seek to avoid.

Negativity is not an overnight phenomenon. Many carefree youths have morphed into grouchy or sad adults due to a lifetime of collected bad vibes. Some people never get over the bullying they experienced as a youngster and spend their entire adult lives trying to make amends.

Death by negativity, really. Your current existence and any hope for a better future are both doomed if you dwell in negativity. The negative attracts the negative.

Negativity can originate from within as well as outside. It's true that some naysayers and individuals wish to bring you down to their level. The sad truth is that most people don't cheer for the success of those they consider close but will cheer on the negative that they have spoken and believe about you. Negativity, however, is not limited to external sources. Your own mind may be a breeding ground for pessimism, feeding doubts about your value, potential, and skills.

The question then becomes how to silence the clamor.

The worst of your setbacks are what you can learn the most from.

No one ever succeeds at everything they try. When you fall short, it hurts like hell. As part of a paradigm of primitive biological cues and responses, your thoughts do everything they can to help you avoid pain and maximize pleasure. It takes courage to try and fail at something. Pain and failure are your greatest gifts, despite how difficult it is to endure them.

However, the agony of failure, or the prospective anguish of failure, can be amplified when you are surrounded by negativity. Fear of failure can prevent you from trying new things, even though you haven't actually failed at anything. Not only does the mind create anxiety to protect you from distress, but so do your social networks. But you are the one to finally alter that.

The most significant lessons you have learned came from the things you tried and failed at. Even though you have experienced substantial grief because of a previous failure, that agony might serve as motivation for future successes. Occasionally, life gives you a lesson that can help you better understand the world around you. While setbacks in the workplace, personal life, or financial situation hurt, they can turn out to be the best things that have ever happened to you.

When you experience setbacks and encounter criticism from inside and without, it's easy to feel like you will never be able to reach your goals. When you start to question your abilities, your thoughts naturally go to a myriad of reasons why you shouldn't pursue a particular aim in the first place. There are always good reasons not to pursue a dream or hope that you once desired. But you must accept that this is par for the course; it eventually strikes everyone.

Setbacks are the steppingstones to future achievements. Long-term success is unachievable without occasional setbacks. The foundation for a wonderful future is laid with the help of setbacks. For those who have had recent or past setbacks, it is imperative to remember that each setback was "simply the opportunity to begin again, this time more intelligibly."

Don't Look at the Negates.

In the face of setbacks, how do you proceed toward success? How can you shut out criticism and push past your own limitations?

The first step is learning the "Why."

It makes no difference how many bad vibes there are in the world. No matter how many times you have tried and failed, keep trying. The reason you want something is what really matters. What motivated you to set or pursue this objective? The first and most crucial step in achieving any goal is determining why you want to achieve it in the first place.

Whenever you set a goal, always start with the why. Lacking a compelling cause to persist in the face of adversity makes it difficult to rise above setbacks and hurt. You can do anything when your "why" is powerful enough. If you can find the underlying cause of why you desire something, and if the answer is meaningful enough, it will serve as a source of motivation while you work toward your goals.

The second step is to grasp the "When."

Knowing when you will reach your goals is the second stage to accomplishing them despite the presence of formidable obstacles, negative feedback, or previous failures. You need to set a date on when you expect to complete your objective. Don't make up some arbitrary time limit. Use precise language.

After justifying your plans to yourself, indicate the date by which you want to accomplish each of your goals. Don't make empty promises that you will diet more this year. Define how much weight you want to lose, why you want to lose it, and by when you want to achieve your goal.

What makes the "when" component crucial?

When you commit to a deadline and put it in writing where you will see it every day, your mind has a funny way of putting pressure on you to get the job done. It's a wonderful prompt to get back on track after encountering setbacks. Be sure to include a timeline with the "what" and "why" of your goals.

The third step is to silence the distractions.

By employing some basic strategies, you may silence the voices of both internal and external negativity. Realize first that there will always be naysayers. It's inevitable that you will encounter naysayers who insist that you can't do anything. You will always have some seed of pessimism growing in the back of your mind. Once you do, you will be well on your way to silencing all the external and internal distractions.

Second, identify what motivates you to create. In the past, many people tried and failed before finally succeeding. The first two enterprises Henry Ford started failed; the first novel Stephen King wrote was rejected by 30 publishers, it took Thomas Edison over 10,000 attempts to design an electric lightbulb that could be sold commercially, and Abraham Lincoln failures were broad and numerous. He failed multiple times in business attempts, then marched into the political realm, where he launched several failed runs at political office before, he became President. He shared this quote that captures my attention "My great concerns is not whether you failed, but whether you are content with failure."

Find whatever it is that motivates you and learn from them. Find out what obstacles stood in their way. Look into the backgrounds of everyone who has ever told you that you can't do something. Keep in mind that setbacks are evidence of growth. If you fail, so what? Isn't it true that you get what you put in? If you have compelling arguments, then yes, of course, it is.

The fourth step is perseverance.

The final and most important step in attaining your goals despite setbacks is tenacity. The route of least resistance never leads to success when it comes to reaching your goals when it comes to soaring to greater heights. Don't kid yourself into thinking that achieving a significant objective will be simple; you will feel like giving up and giving in to your failures and frustrations. When that happens, you have to keep your nose to the grindstone.

Keep in mind that many others before you have tried and failed many times before succeeding. Realize that it will be difficult to achieve your goals in life, no matter what they are (more money, a better-paying job, weight loss, achieving a worthwhile goal, growing a business, etc.). You need to continue making an effort till you get there. You will have setbacks and criticism from all sides, but you must keep trying. As time goes on, you will get closer and closer to your objectives if you keep at it.

Your aspirations and dreams are worth fighting for, no matter what. If you put your mind to it, you can achieve your wildest dreams. If you have an adventurous attitude, you will reap an adventurous reward, but it won't be simple.

DAY 20
GOD WILL HEAL YOUR BROKENNESS

A broken heart may result from rejection, abuse, trauma, or any other painful life experience. The end outcome may be resentment or even despair. Your struggles may cause your heart to become hard and indifferent to God, preventing you from enjoying his blessings.

If you are feeling broken, it is because you have been kicked so hard and so often that you are barely a shell of your former self. You are completely alone and secluded. No one notices or can help you out of this pit of despair. When you are in agony on this scale, it might make you feel like you can't breathe, can't move, and can't experience the pleasure in life that you once did.

Despair wears a certain face like the glass has been shattered. The items were crumpled into a heap. The edges snapped, and something ripped. Brokenness contaminates everything it touches. It has an unrefined, broken appearance. As soon as you see it, you understand. When it's genuine, you can feel it.

That doesn't mean you can treat every broken item the same. Ignoring broken bones is difficult. However, there are certain things that are not as difficult to handle as a broken bone. In order for brokenness to get your attention, it often takes a huge event. You will realize that those who inhabit a broken world become accustomed to its brokenness; they accept it, sing a cheerful song, and get on with their lives.

You can be aware of how broken the system is and yet, you still go about your daily lives in a state of denial about how broken everything really is.

In some cases, that may be desirable, but you shouldn't dwell only on the negative. That's not the Christian way to live, and it's not the way anyone should try to live either *(1 Timothy 4:4)*.

However, you can't fix the problem until you identify it. Humor can't prevent tears forever. You might anticipate experiencing unforeseen hardships in your life, and when that occurs, you know that time alone cannot mend your wounds; you must look beyond the grave for a source of comfort. All sinners end up crying, but as the righteous, you have solutions because you are not average folks who occasionally have a bad day. God's grace is all you have as broken humans.

Jesus can relate to your brokenness. He is familiar with the pain of deceit and scorn. Someone distorted His words. People said demons possessed him. He was subjected to physical torture before being crucified. His life was flawless, but his death was gruesome. However, Jesus was always obedient to God, allowing Him to triumph over His brokenness. Therefore, on the third day after his death, Jesus rose from the grave and is still alive today. By surrendering His life to the Father, He made the decision to be healed by God.

Getting healing from brokenness

Where do you go when the pain of your own brokenness becomes too much to bear, and you don't know if you can make it through another day? To the Suffering Servant, of whom it is written, *"A bruised reed he will not break, and a faintly burning wick he will not quench" (Isaiah 42:3)*. He is a kind Healer who can help you get well again.

You may learn to trust a new side of God, as Job did in his moment of severe brokenness *(Job 9:22-24)*. Perhaps you might be thinking; God enjoys seeing you in pain. You might think His affection for you isn't as strong as you have always assumed. When you don't know what's causing your pain or can't point to a specific sin or an area of spiritual development, you can feel helpless and hopeless. What does it say about God's nature when life suffers for no apparent reason? Does God take your suffering into account?

God is not out to further fracture you; He is focused on your restoration. However, more breaks are occasionally necessary for proper bone healing. It doesn't mean God doesn't care if your life is falling apart. God does not love to see you forever broken. He's patching up problems you didn't know existed. He's performing feats that only God can. When a bone is broken, new tissue grows between the fractures. When you come to God with a broken heart, His Spirit reaches down and heals you.

Everyone who is suffering can find comfort. The Almighty up there is all-seeing and all-knowing. He listened to the plight of the Israelites as they were enslaved *(Exodus 2:24)*. He witnessed Hagar's weeping *(Genesis 21:17)*, Hannah's *(I Samuel 1:10–11)*, and David's *(Psalms 6:6–9)*. *(Psalm 56:8)*, says that he put them all in his jar. *(Psalm 147:3)*, says that God is close to the hurting and helps them heal.

The God of the universe is more than just omniscient; He is a responder, too. All this suffering is for your own good, though. It will add to the splendor *(2 Corinthians 4:17)*. God's grace and mercy will shine brighter in light of your brokenness. You may never know Jesus is all you need until Jesus is all you have, and this is something you won't really grasp until you have reached your own personal rock bottom.

Take a peek at the final chapter. God doesn't eliminate the things from our lives that we wish He would. When God finally brings heaven to earth at the end of time, he doesn't delete everything and starts again. He fixes it up instead. There will be peace on earth when wolves and lambs graze together, lions eat straw like oxen, and snakes eat dirt. *"In my entire holy mountain they shall not hurt or destroy"* (Isaiah 65:25). Whether it's the planet, His creation, or you personally, if you put your faith in Him He will fix it. Despite its current state of disrepair, the future of our planet seems promising.

Your pain may seem insurmountable right now. That's right; I can relate. But remember that there is a God in the heavens whose job is to fix the broken. Perhaps the depth of your despair is beyond words. Your entire world has collapsed. You are stuck in the present and fear the future. There seems to be no escape route available to you. The hole is blocked since the rock was rolled over it. Darkness, it's been a while.

However, hope does exist. One can be saved. Someone is aware of the location of your grave. They also incarcerated him. Jesus is a God with an empathetic understanding of human suffering. He died on the cross, but now he lives again. Now he is leaving to create a home for you where wounds can be mended, children will prophesy, the aged will see visions, and the young will be given dreams. Anyone who puts their faith in the Lord will be saved, according to (*Joel 2:28 and 32*).

Some dark abyss may have broken you. Actually, who isn't? However, as Corrie ten Boom so eloquently put it, "No pit is so deep that He is not deeper still; with Jesus, even in our darkest moments, the best remains, and the very best is yet to be."

"The Great Physician," called Jesus. "Those who are well have no need for a physician, but those who are sick. It's good for a person to accept the fact that they're really broken, and they should never stay that way. Jesus, the Great Physician, has the power to heal you from all your brokenness. I am a testimony of being healed from brokenness by the Great Physician called Jesus.

DAY 21

DON'T GET STUCK IN YOUR PAST

I know you are familiar with phrases like: "Don't get stuck in the past," "Don't dwell in the past," "Let the ghost rest in the past," etc. What do these phrases imply, and how does it affect your soaring to a greater height? We will discuss this in this section; welcome on board!

To avoid being stuck in your past, you must charge headfirst into the future. Seize each day as a chance to take another step toward the good things God has in store for you and view each obstacle as a mountain to be conquered rather than a boulder that will crush you.

If your past is holding you back, you won't be able to completely embrace the bright future that lies ahead of you. If you let it, your memories might prevent you from living in the moment and reaping the benefits of your present and future. God wants you to turn away from your past and look ahead with excitement and confidence, and the surest way to reach new heights and keep going even when things look bleak is to refuse to live in the past.

God is committed to delivering you from your past. The Biblical account of Lot's wife is perhaps the best example of this. Let's study that story.

Lot and his family were residents of a city overrun by evil and vice. God was so incensed by the filth in this city and a neighboring one that He decided to wipe them both off the face of the earth. He dispatched two angels to Lot's home to warn him to grab his family and get out of there. Angels cried out, "Run for your lives!" as they surrounded them. Escape to the mountains [of Moab] lest you be burned; do not look back or stop anywhere in the valley." *(Genesis 19:17, emphasis added)*. The wife of Lot disobeyed the order not to look back into the past. She suddenly became a pillar of salt.

Jesus emphasized the importance of not forgetting this incident when Jesus comments in *(Luke 17:32), where He said, "Remember Lot's wife."* What He meant by that was, "Don't bother looking back. Time in the past is over. Don't be stuck in the past; start planning for the future!

You will never feel like you have a future if you dwell on the past. God will provide one, but you may miss it if you hold on to the past and refuse to let the ghost of the past rest in peace.

Looking back can obscure your vision of the future. You feel down, dejected, and hopeless. Don't act as though the things that have happened to you in the past are more significant than what lies ahead of you. Doing so will leave you stuck in the past, robbing you of the joy of living in the here and now and the optimism of going forward to the future. Lot's wife perished because she turned to look back. She had to leave her home and her future behind. I don't want you to lose yourself by remembering the past. Even if you don't actually transform into a pillar of salt, dwelling too much on the past might make you feel as "dead" as if you were sitting in a mound of salt.

Focusing on the past will lead to more of the same, but looking to the future will help me get closer to God's plan for my life. There's no need to live in fear of making the same mistakes twice. You can do better in the future with the support of God's spiritual energy, strength, and grace while believing that God is greater than your sins, mistakes, and shortcomings. The failures of the past have no place in your hopes for the future. They'll make you feel sluggish and trapped.

Many mornings, the enemy starts to bring up everything that went wrong or did not go as planned the day before, even before your feet hit the floor. The adversary wants to utilize your past to prevent you from enjoying your present. He's always looking for methods to turn the tables on you. But God does not want us to be slaves to the past.

If you choose to see it that way, each day can be a fresh start. God's grace is bigger than your sins of the past. The opponent wants to use your memories to prevent you from enjoying the present. Daily, God's mercies begin again. You must declare out, "God's mercies are new every morning," when you awaken, and Satan begins reading you an inventory of yesterday's failings. God, I accept Your mercy currently. Forgive me, and I thank You. I appreciate Your help in letting go of the past so that I can go on to a bright future. Say to yourself, "Something good is going to happen to me today!" instead of dreading the worst that could happen today.

Being pessimistic depletes the energy of everyone involved, but having hope, faith, and an optimistic outlook allows God to perform miracles. Only you can stop the opponent from talking about the past. No one else can take care of it for you. You'll have to learn to give the devil a piece of your mind if you want to win the battle and go forward into the great future God has prepared for you. No one can lend you their willpower; you must find it within yourself and declare, "I am born to soar!" My enemy will not be able to exploit my past and use it against me. I refuse to let yesterday determine my happiness in the present! Getting where you're supposed to go requires you to let go of the past.

Don't think about your previous transgressions, past failures, past mistakes, past associates, past lifestyle, former nature, past occupation, etc. You must prevent your thoughts from returning to such "former things."

When you repent, do you honestly think God would overlook your sins? Indeed, he does. Once you have repented, you no longer need to feel guilty or condemned for your previous actions. To take this a step further, I want you to know that God doesn't just forgive you for your faults; He also forgets them.

God emphasizes His forgiveness of sins throughout the Old and New Testaments. Specifically, He promises in *(Jeremiah 31:34), "For I will forgive their iniquity, and I will [seriously] remember their sin no more."* (Hebrews 10:17), *"And their sins and their lawbreaking I will remember no more."*

When Jesus died on the cross two thousand years ago, He forgave your past sins and promised to forgive your future sins as well. Everything bad you will ever do is already planned for by God, from the thoughts that cross your mind to the words that will come out of your mouth. Keeping in touch with Him is all that's required.

The price of your past has been paid.

The enemy enjoys bringing up unpleasant memories. Like a broken record, he repeats the errors, let-downs hurt, and offenses of the past over and over in your head. You have to pay for everything you've done wrong. Expenses are on you! Expenses are on you! Put up or shut up!

Please don't ever give up your future to "pay" for your mistakes of the past. The false belief that a terrible past precludes a good future is something you should not buy into. Don't let yourself fall into the trap of thinking your past failures mean there's no chance for a better future.

To encourage you and offer you hope for your future, God declares in *(Jeremiah 29:11), "For I know the plans I have for you, says the Lord. They are plans for good and not for disaster, to give a future and hope."* Believe that God has excellent plans for you, no matter what your past may entail. Even if you mess up, this will still be true. It's only not true for you if you want to believe otherwise. You can't make something happen for yourself if you don't think it's possible. God's thoughts and designs for you are for your welfare and peace, not for evil, regardless of your past, but this will only become clear to you if you choose to believe it and hold on to that belief despite any circumstances. You may have faith in your future because He is on your side and has wonderful things for you. Your future is bright in Christ, "LET GO THE PAST!"

DAY 22

I AM NOT YOUR ENEMY; IT'S SPIRITUAL

Battling against the darkness and answering the call to resist the enemy (the devil) is spiritual warfare. In this section, we will look at the teachings of the Apostle Paul in *Ephesians 6:10-12* and how you might apply them to your experience of soaring.

(*Ephesians 6:10-12*)

"A final word: Be strong with the Lord's mighty power. Put on all of God's armor so that you will be able to stand firm against all strategies and tricks of the Devil. For we are not fighting against people made of flesh and blood, but against the evil rulers and authorities of the unseen world, against those mighty powers of darkness who rule this world, and against wicked spirits in the heavenly realms."

"Be strong in the Lord and His might."

Finally, at the conclusion of the letter, Paul lays out the fundamentals of the Christian life after carefully establishing his position in relation to Jesus. This is the last part of his writing that discusses the walk. Paul speaks in light of what he has said thus far since he is writing this letter at this point.

Considering the behavior God expects of each believer, the filling of the Holy Spirit, and your walk in the Spirit, living a Christian life involves fighting spiritual warfare. He continued by saying that every Christian must have strength in the Lord and His might: Paul actually said, "Strengthen yourself in the Lord." Since soaring on the wings of an eagle is more of a spiritual exercise, and if you are not strong, you can be hindered and continue living less of who you are, you must be spiritually empowered to soar.

You must first be strong in the Lord and in the power of His might, according to the thorough instruction on spiritual warfare in this verse. You must then put on all of God's protective armor. Both are crucial, but a lot of teaching on Christian combat ignores the first. Even if you put the best armor on a frail man who can hardly stand, he will still be a useless soldier. He'll be defeated with ease. Therefore, the guiding principle of "be strong in the Lord and in the power of His might" must come first when preparing for spiritual warfare.

Being strong in the Lord is comparable to a soldier going through training before heading to the front lines of battle. A soldier must complete basic training before being given a pistol or being shown how to launch a missile. Increasing the recruit's physical strength is an excellent reason for basic training. It's as if the military is telling the soldier, "Soldier, we're going to provide you with the best armor and weaponry we can. However, we must first make sure that you are capable of using what we offer you and that you are powerful." The same principle applies to the spiritual realm; you must first be prepared for battle before you can stand your ground against the myriad forces of evil that will try to prevent your soaring. Let's move on to the verse's subsequent phrase.

And "In the might of His power." This demonstrates how to gain the power required to soar. Saying these words alone won't cause this to occur. It is not a magic or an incantation. Simply repeating, "Be strong in the Lord and in the power of His might," won't make anything happen.

It might refer to innate strength or force. Even if a man doesn't use his large muscles, they nonetheless show his strength. It is the store of power.

Power is used to exercise strength. The strong man employs his power when he uses his force to bend an iron bar. It indicates that the reserve of power is truly being used.

God possesses immeasurable reserves of power that can be felt as strength in every Christian's life. But while you are sitting still, His power is not at work in you. His power manifests itself in you as you rely on it and go about your task, just like an eagle uses a storm thermal to take flight. You can either do nothing or rely on His might, or you may work with your strength and not rely on His power. The best you can do with your strength is run or fly, but both will fall short, and you won't soar to greater heights. For this reason, you must first rely on His strength before beginning the task.

Relying on God's power does not mean "I do everything, and God does nothing." It doesn't mean, "I do nothing, and God does everything." It is not "I do everything I can, and God fills in the gaps for me." All of those approaches are wrong. The secret is for you to labor by faith while relying on His power increasingly.

The Apostle Paul's next instruction in this verse is "To put on all of God's armor."

"Put on the whole armor of God" God provides a complete arsenal for the believer, and He sends you into war with all you require.

Only once does this ancient Greek term armor appear in the New Testament. Jesus describes a strong guy who is fully armed but loses all his armor when a stronger person overpowers him *(Luke 11:21–22)*. According to *(Colossians 2:15)*, Jesus destroyed all principalities and powers.

Both in a sense that armor comes from God and that it is God's protection for His children, this armor is of God. The Lord accordingly wears the armor too *(Isaiah 59:17)*. He now gives us access to that armor. We are more than conquerors because we are clad in God's armor *(Romans 8:37)*.

What do you do with the armor now that you have it on? "…So that you may be able to resist the devil's schemes." By resisting the devil's wiles, you can only demonstrate the power you have in God. Satan's plans for you are foiled when you stand against them in God's might.

(Ephesians 6:12) says, "For we do not wrestle against things that are made of flesh and blood, but against things that are ruled by spiritual hosts of wickedness in heavenly places."

Because you fight against principalities and powers instead of flesh and blood: Paul did not command the believer to engage in spiritual combat.

You do not wrestle against flesh and blood, but (you do wrestle) against principalities, and so forth, he simply said as fact. Your struggle is spiritual. You are probably losing the battle if you are unaware of or ignore this truth.

Because you do not fight against actual people: Many Christians focus all of their energies on fighting flesh and blood, forgetting that this is not their true war. Paul's point in this passage is similar to his point in (*2 Corinthians 10:3-4*), "*For even though we are made of flesh, we do not fight like it. Because they are powerful in God and not made of flesh, our weapons of war can overthrow strongholds.*"

According to this scripture, the major goal of spiritual battle and the armor of God is to enable you to soar. It is impossible to resist the assaults of spiritual foes without the might of God and the defense of spiritual armor.

In order for you to endure the bad day and have done everything to stand, this explains the function of God's might and his armor as well as how you should employ them. God has assigned His people a task, a mission, and a path to follow. Satan will make every effort to thwart it. You are to stand your ground when he strikes and threatens. Paul clearly places emphasis on this in (*Ephesians 6:11 and 6:13*). You carry out the will of the Lord and resist any hints of spiritual opposition.

DAY 23

YOU ARE IN THE ROOM OF GREATNESS

Superiority, extreme beauty, splendor, and still another term, greatness, are a few synonyms for the word "excellence." Excellence and greatness can be used interchangeably. What then is greatness? Greatness refers to "exceeding others." To put it in another way, greatness helps you outperform others.

This helps us comprehend great individuals like Abraham and David. Since excellence and greatness are synonymous, Abraham and David were both wonderful people. Excellence also refers to having extraordinary discretion and superb perception. The distinction between the greats and the smalls is that many people lack awareness of their surroundings and other people's needs. Tremendous individuals have tremendous visions, and great visions don't necessarily entail lofty goals or plans but rather a remarkable amplitude of perception—the capacity to take in a lot at once. You will always see greatness whenever you see an eagle because they always stand out among all birds.

God's Spirit teaches us to be good in a variety of ways. He sometimes trains you for greatness by using seemingly little things. Imagine entering a space and discovering a glass cup perched precariously on a table. A great person will act right now to stop the cup from shattering. God can trust you to save people if you can save a cup that was placed in a perilous position. You will be more likely to spot danger and take action to safeguard others. Regularly showing greatness in major endeavors won't be difficult if you do so in the minor things.

You have greatness within of you, but if your life gets too busy, it can prevent your abilities from developing, so make room for excellence.

You don't have room for fresh encounters, better chances, or rising greatness when your life is overstuffed.

Sometimes, in order to grasp something better, you must be willing to let go of what you already have.

When you are experiencing worry and fear, it will be difficult for you to dream, be creative, or push yourself outside your comfort zone.

There won't be room for forgiveness, grace, or understanding when you're in a relationship that is characterized by mistrust.

Your life will not be full of contentment, fulfillment, and purpose if it is full of disappointment.

What part of your life needs greater development? Is it your spirit, mind, heart, connections, soul, joy, or peace?

You make room for greatness to enter your life when you make space in these areas. It may manifest as fresh chances, new connections, fresh ideas, and fresh routines. Be expectant, if you expect nothing, you will get nothing. As prepare adequately to achieve greatness, God will give you His divine strength through His son Jesus Christ. *In the book of (Isaiah 40: 26), "He calls them by name, by the greatness of His might, and because he is strong in power, not one is lacking."*

Refuse to lead a life that is so packed with obligations that it is unproductive. Living a crammed life will only keep your opportunities scarce. Decide to create space for excellence today. Don't be found among those that settle for mediocrity.

In the book of (Psalms 71: 21-23), "Thou shalt increase my greatness, and comfort me on every side. I will also praise thee with the psaltery even thy truth, O thou Holy One of Israel. My lips shall greatly rejoice when I sing unto thee; And my soul which thou hast redeemed." Once you put your faith and trust in God, consistently relying on Him as the author and finisher of your faith; He will increase you in all areas of your life.

Greatness in the Bible was never determined by how much money someone had or how much influence or power they claimed to have. Greatness was always given to the one who has surrendered all to God and accepts Jesus Christ as Lord and Saviour; and once you're willing to walk and fulfill your God's given purpose for His glory.

Today God is calling you into the room of greatness to fulfill your God's given purpose in Jesus' name Amen.

DAY 24

IF GOD SAID IT! HE WILL DO IT!

Does God speak? Does God do whatever He says? Do you think God tells lies? The book of *(Hebrews 6:18) says, "It is impossible for God to lie."* God *"is not a man that He should lie, nor the son of man that He should repent,"* according to *(Numbers 23:19)*. God assured Israel, in His word in *(Isaiah 55:11), that His word will not come back void.* Do you also believe this?

These scriptural truths imply that you should always believe, trust, and obey God's word. You must keep in mind as we explore this matter that God always follows through on His promises. He says what He means, which is why this should prompt you to exercise greater caution in your interactions with Him and in all that you do.

Be adamant about your belief in what God has said. Never cast any doubt on God's Word; don't let any clouds or maybes cover it. Set it aside. The psalmist states in *(Psalm 119:89), "Forever, O LORD, thy word is settled in heaven."* The word of God is firmly established in Heaven, which means it is also firmly established for you here on Earth. God has spoken it; all you need to do is believe it. Once you do, the matter is resolved, and you can rely on the promises in His Word to bring about your needs.

You must learn how to put your faith into action; simply having it is not enough. You must then learn how to employ the things God offers you. Why do you believe the Holy Spirit was sent to baptize and indwell those who have experienced new birth? He is also here to assist you, instruct you, and lead you in making use of the resources God has made available to you right here on Earth.

God proclaims that, He will meet all your needs. However, according to his riches in glory in Christ Jesus, my God will meet all your needs *(Philippians 4:19)*. How many individuals genuinely think God will care for all their needs? How many people still have trouble accepting God's amazing promises? I have faith in God's promises to provide for all my needs. It's settled because God, not man, said it.

Are you pacing the floor while wringing your hands and contemplating your next move? You were told to trust God. God proclaimed through His Holy Word: *"Trust in the LORD with all thy heart, and do not lean unto thy own understanding." Recognize Him in all your deeds, and he will guide your steps (Proverbs 3:5-6).* This implies that God will provide your necessities. He wouldn't ask you to follow His courses and then fail to provide for your needs after you did. He creates clear roads for you to travel on and uses His grace and strength to help you along those paths. He guides you along holy, upright roads that are ripe with the fruits of goodness and mercy. All along those roads, he provides a plentiful supply. Take what He offers freely.

Why do you remain up all night in terror, sobbing, dreading what will happen when the day rises, and worrying about how you will meet your needs? The Lord said He would meet your needs. Set it aside in your head. You struggle and hope when you don't allow the promises of God to become tangible enough for you to accept the outcomes in your mind; nonetheless, struggling and hoping does not equate to believing.

What has the Lord spoken concerning you? His words have never failed, and they won't fail now, don't be afraid once He has said it! He will do it!

DAY 25

DON'T LIVE IN DEFEAT

Failure is a common occurrence in our world. The Bible even states in *(James 3:2) that, "We all make mistakes in various ways."* I want to warn everyone right now that this does not give us the freedom to live recklessly, as if nothing is important. This does not imply that we should disregard common sense and lead carefree lives. James is merely highlighting a universal truth, namely that everyone will fail at something at some point in their lives. Some people have experienced more failures than accomplishments. I also want to emphasize that we are to live by God's established norm. So once more, we are not free to disregard prudence and lead our chosen life. James is letting you know that you should expect to make mistakes, stumble, and fail in life. Those who assume and believe that you can live all your life without ever making a mistake are the ones who are mostly affected by their failures.

We all experience setbacks, failures, defeats, and losses in life. Nobody is flawless. Everyone makes errors. If you do not properly address or manage your failures and setbacks in life with the proper attitude and frame of mind, they can have a catastrophic impact on your life. In truth, you can experience the same kinds of setbacks and failures that Job had. *(Job 17:11) states, "My days are past; my purposes, even the ideas in my heart, have been severed."* Who is Job talking to? Job is expressing his pain; this expression can also mean, "It's over, my hope is gone, my heart's aspirations are gone, and my dreams are broken. There is nothing more I can do." Have you ever experienced something

like this? Have you ever thought that your life was over after experiencing a failure or defeat? Have you ever had the feeling that all hope for the future was lost? Have you ever had the feeling that your hopes and goals were crushed? You are a member of the human race if you have ever experienced having your hopes for the future dashed and your aspirations crushed. I know you will feel defeated when things like this happen, but it doesn't have to go that way. If you can just learn how to Deal with Defeat, you can overcome those feelings of failure and defeat and move on to a better future.

In the words of John Maxwell, he said, "The difference between average people and achieving people is their perception of and response to failure." In other words, those who succeed in life have a positive outlook on failure. They improve themselves because of their experience and ability to see past their failure to the future.

Everyone goes through a training process of failure to succeed. In other words, neither you nor I will achieve without experiencing some level of failure along the road. The good news is that your failure need not be catastrophic or irreparable.

You must realize that failing to complete a task does not equate to failure. Failure is defined by someone's inability to stand up and try again. It's important to keep in mind that your failures are not final, and just because you fail at something does not make you a failure.

You must also keep in mind that God is not startled by your shortcomings. "Peter responded and said unto him, though all men shall be offended because of thee, yet will I never be offended; Jesus' remark to him in *(Matthew 26:33-34)* indicates that Jesus was aware of and foretold Peter's denial and failure. God is not surprised by your shortcomings. Considering that, let's examine how to overcome defeat.

How to Overcome Defeat

1. Take Ownership of Your Failure: According to *(Proverbs 28:13), "He who covers his sins shall not prosper; but he who acknowledges and repents of them shall find mercy."*

The first step to overcoming defeat is taking ownership of your life. You are accountable for your behavior, words, attitudes, and responses to other people as well as to life itself. Nobody else is to blame for your flaws and failures in life. Shifting blame and pointing the finger at someone else is much simpler.

You will have to answer for your life when you stand before God, not someone else's. Admit your mistakes if you have done so. I failed. I was mistaken. Face it head-on. Be truthful to yourself. Deal with others fairly. "I was mistaken," Over the years, I've come to realize that I have no influence over what people do to me or say about me. I can, however, choose how I respond to and react to them. I must respond in a way that pleases God. I must take ownership of my life and my contribution to my failure and loss.

2. Stop Worrying and Begin to Repent: Don't let the past hold you captive. By letting go of it, you can escape from it. Many people's pasts serve as prisons. They are the ones who keep saying, "If I had done this" or "If I had done that," so you would recognize them. I wouldn't be in this situation if I had just made better decisions. These individuals are held captive by their past. The definitions of repent include changing one's mind and changing one's course. In other words, take action to overcome your setback.

(2 Corinthians 7:10), "For godly sorrow works repentance to salvation not to be repented of: but the sorrow of the world works death."

This verse distinguishes between two types of sadness: sorrow toward God and sorrow toward the world. What's the distinction? You are inspired to change by godly sorrow. It causes a shift in perspective. It inspires you to take constructive action. "I'll make a change. I'll do things differently. I've come to my senses. I'll take what I can from it. If you're going to fail, try to do so wisely. It inspires you to make a change.

Worldly sorrow kills and is sad and disheartening. I'm really sorry. Self-pity is among the most damaging feelings a person may have. "I have failed. I am useless. Nothing I do is right. Everyone despises me, and nobody likes me. "Oh, poor me!" This is worldly sorrow.

Stop feeling sorry. Regret doesn't make anything different. It only serves to keep you gazing backward. It's comparable to trying to drive while staring in the rear-view mirror.

3. Pay attention to the future: I strive to finish the race and win the prize for which God, through Christ Jesus, is calling us up to heaven, putting the past behind me and focusing on the future. This is the word of the Apostle Paul.

For you to overcome defeat, too, you need to start where you are right now and decide that a successful future is your goal.

4. Put your future in God's hands: *(Joel 2:25) "I will make up the years that the locusts have destroyed."* A fresh start begins with restored confidence in God. Defeat has a way of making your faith difficult. Your faith may, at times, be tested beyond its capacity. God needs to be the absolute focus of your life. God desires for both you and me to lead successful Christian lives. But you can only do it if you put your faith in Him for the future. God wants to make up for the time lost to failure and defeat. He wants to replace your ashes with beauty, and you're grieving with joy by giving you these things.

You don't need to accept loss, and you don't need to let it destroy you. You may turn defeat into victory by understanding what leads to failure and how it affects your life, then react constructively.

DAY 26
PUT AN END TO PROCRASTINATION

D o you think a procrastinator can soar? When you procrastinate, you never see a perfect time to start a thing. Procrastination may completely consume your life, forcing you to put off important and less important tasks. What should you do when procrastination, the slothful demon, tries to infiltrate your life? You must put an end to procrastination. Eagles don't procrastinate; if you are going to soar on an eagle's wing, you need to get rid of procrastination.

If you're a meteorologist, there's nothing wrong with spending excessive time examining the wind and clouds. However, there is much wrong with it if you observe the wind and clouds to avoid performing the task that needs to be done. It's also possible that you will put off a task you hate doing forever if you wait impatiently for the "perfect time" to complete it.

Decide to get up and move about right this second. Just take the first step toward realizing your objective. After taking a step, you are engaged in and working on the process.

Doing what you need to do when you need to do it has a nice and "right" quality, a strong item, a liberating force, and a positive feeling that inspires confidence.

Procrastination is a Time Thief.

What can you learn about procrastination from the Bible? Is there any information on this kind of behavior in the Bible? Yes. Procrastination is one of the many behavioral issues that the Bible truly addresses. Blessings are destroyed by procrastination. You can lose your sense of self-worth, dependability, and tranquillity. The Bible states in *(Proverbs 18:9) "He also who is slack in his work Is brother to him who destroys."*

Putting things off frequently is a sign of a lack of self-control. Self-control, also known as temperance, is one of the fruits of the spirit, according to Galatians 5:23. The Holy Spirit gives you power when you learn to live in the spirit. The Bible teaches that while Satan can exert influence over your body, your spirit has the power to overcome him and regain control over it. You are able to overcome your fleshly shortcomings because of the strength of the Holy Spirit. The human spirit can be drawn upon to transcend any and all fleshly cravings or infirmities, just as fasting and prayer enable you to transcend and momentarily suspend your fleshly impulses and need for nourishment and procrastination is one of those fleshy impulses that the Holy Spirit can help you suspend.

Procrastination is the act of delaying both major and minor tasks.

It's possible to get so adept at putting things off that your to-do list grows to such an extent that it causes tension. This is because you continued putting things off. You should be aware that procrastination has become a significant disadvantage by the time you reach this "black belt" level and that it is time to make a change. The act of procrastination causes a blockage in its chronic stages. It makes it impossible to accomplish anything. Instead of allowing for the setting of one item ahead of accomplishing another, it turns into a mental brick wall that can grow strong and is hard to get through.

Why do we occasionally let ourselves build such a wall? Is it primarily just plain old laziness? Or does fear tend to be the main culprit? The worry that doing a task would affect your life, and you simply don't like the thought of change.

I am not referring to a significant life shift. I am referring to commonplace activities that can even slightly alter how you typically do your daily activities. The basement or garage can be cleaned up and organized to help you forget about "the way things were." I think that sometimes, your fear of change might manifest itself in the strict control over your personal space, something you can control, even though you may not even be aware of it.

How can you break these harmful habits? Is it really necessary for you to involve God in something that can seem so unimportant? Even though it may appear unimportant, procrastination has several negative effects on your life. Below are some effects of procrastination.

1. Procrastinating tasks or projects that are crucial to your profession, family, or personal life can prevent others from succeeding by not doing your part.

2. You attempt to avoid choosing or committing to something vital or required.

3. Procrastination makes you take part regularly in time-wasting, health-harming activities (such as being a couch potato who avoids exercise).

4. You frequently arrive late for appointments or carelessly put off taking care of financial responsibilities.

5. Procrastination makes you pressure people to accomplish your chores or responsibilities.

Reaching out to God might be just what you need to do if you want to stop procrastinating and don't think you can accomplish it on your own. You must ask God to be present in all aspects of your life, big and small if you want His talents to be stirred up. Who knows what you might be able to do after you learn to quit putting things off once you break your procrastination habit?

Procrastination Can Be Ended

Remember that you will encounter physical and mental difficulties as long as you remain in your physical body. You are psychologically and physically bound to the weaknesses and temptations of flesh since your body is constituted of it. This makes it impossible to entirely conquer any of your limitations. There will always be some conflict between your spirit and your flesh. You can only expect to lead a life that provides you access to spiritual strength so that God will empower you each day to overcome your limits and frailties as humans.

Procrastination and its cousin, blame, are both ridiculous, but it's important to remember that this is not something to be laughed at. When you put off till tomorrow what you must or ought to do today, you really overwhelm tomorrow and waste a significant portion of today. You also refuse to exercise control over your spirit, putting off your blessings and showing a lack of self-discipline. There is no way, in my opinion, that God could approve of procrastination; this is why you must put an end to it.

DAY 27
TAKE HOLD OF YOUR VICTORY BECAUSE GRACE WINS

Victory in life goes beyond physical prowess. Victory in destiny is not inversely related to ability. To be victorious in life, you undoubtedly need intelligence, unceasing effort, unrivaled diligence, wisdom, and competence. All of these are essential, but they will not bring you the level of victory and prosperity that God has planned for you.

You need a certain component of destiny to win. It is known as Grace. Grace is defined as "The love and mercy we receive from God because God desires that we have it, not because we deserve to earn it."

When grace is absent, distinctiveness is also absent. What remains outside of grace is dishonor, defeat, and disillusionment. Life without grace is frustrating!

Without the Lord, those who construct a house labor in vain, and those who keep watch over a city awake only in vain without the Lord's protection. Builders construct, and guards keep watch! Those are efforts, but they are in vain unless you cooperate with the Lord. But when you have God's grace, everything you do is magnified and produces amazing results.

Many intelligent individuals struggle in life because *"...it is not of him who wills, nor of him who runs, but of God who shows mercy" (Romans 9:16)*. A tiny lad carrying a stone that might not even be able to kill a small bird defeated Goliath, a powerful man of war with years of training and competence could not do it, because he lacks Grace.

The grace of God is available to take over for you and put you where you may ordinarily never get to in life, regardless of how weak you think you are. Nevertheless, if you consider yourself to be a strong man, allow me to remind you that there are people and forces that are stronger than you and that, barring God's grace, you will continue to face difficulties. Without God's support, you cannot impact the world and will be hindered from triumphing and reaching new heights. Soaring is impossible without Grace.

There are diverse acts of Grace; let's quickly discuss them as we conclude this section.

The Diverse Acts of Grace

1. Grace of God brings Salvation to humanity: The ultimate act of God's grace towards us was demonstrated through the sacrifice of Jesus Christ on the cross. Through His death and resurrection, He paid the penalty for our sins and made it possible for us to have eternal life. This is the foundation of our faith and the reason we can have hope in God *(Romans 3: 23-26)*. We are saved by grace through faith in Jesus Christ, not by our own works or efforts. Salvation through faith in Jesus Christ reminds us that our salvation is not dependent on our abilities but on our faith in Christ. *(Ephesians 2: 8-9)*

2. Grace of God brings forgiveness of sins through Jesus Christ: Because of Jesus Christ's sacrifice, we can be forgiven of our sins and made righteous in the eyes of God. This forgiveness is not something that we earn or deserve but is a gift of God's grace. It is a reminder that we cannot earn our salvation through good works, but we must rely on God's grace alone. *(Ephesians 1: 7)*

3. Grace of God steps in when all else fails. God's grace for our shortcomings: We should accept God's grace for our shortcomings. We are not perfect, and we will make mistakes and fall short of God's standards. But through His grace, we can be forgiven and restored. We should not be afraid to come to God with our failures and weaknesses; instead, we should rely on His grace to help us overcome them. *(2 Corinthians 12: 9-10)*

It reminds us that we cannot be defined by our failures or weaknesses but by God's love and grace toward us. God's grace is sufficient; we must depend on him to help us through our struggles.

4. Grace of God allows us to extend grace to others: Just as God has extended grace to us; we should also extend grace to others *(Colossians 3: 13)*. This means forgiving those who have wronged us, mistreated us, abused us, ridiculed us, rejected us, abandoned us, showing kindness to those who are in need, and loving those who are difficult to love. As we extend grace to others, we become a reflection of God's grace in the world.

5. Grace has the power to change one's life: Paul's conversion is the true reflection of God's grace. Before Paul's conversion, he was persecuting the Christians, but God showed up and extended His grace and mercy to Damascus. A bright light blinded him, and Jesus spoke to him, transforming him into one of the greatest Apostles of all time.

What a miracle! *(Acts 9:1-19)* This act of grace is a powerful example of God's transformative power in our lives. This story is a reminder that no one is beyond the reach of God's grace. All you need is grace if you want to prevail in life's fights.

God shows us the extent of His grace through unexpected persons, unexpected circumstances, and illogical timing. Search for God's grace in your life but be prepared for it to manifest itself in unanticipated ways. One way to prepare your heart for God's grace is to wait patiently on Him.

In every season, seek out and abide in God's grace; there will be a bright sky, storms, turbulence, and everything in between in this life. If you're experiencing clear skies, give thanks to God for His mercy. Give God praise for His grace if you are going through a difficult time. If you are going through a stormy time, give God praise for His grace, because you have a beacon that will always lead you to greater heights. That is the grace of God.

DAY 28

TRY AGAIN

It's simple to give up when you attempt something that seems difficult at times, right? I know you have experienced that at times.

Have you ever tried to drive a nail through a substantial, tough board? You cannot simply make one successful attempt before giving up. The nail must penetrate the board; thus, you must keep hammering. Your hand could develop a blister, or the nail could bend, forcing you to start over. Even if it may seem like you aren't making much progress, giving up will prevent the task from being completed, so you must continue to try.

The aforementioned example illustrates persistence. When someone is persistent, it indicates they keep trying over again and over again despite becoming discouraged.

Jesus discusses persistence in the Bible. He instructed his followers to *"always pray, and not give up" (Luke 18:1)*. He shared a story with them to inspire them.

"A woman once approached a judge to ask for help because she didn't think she was being treated fairly. The woman kept returning to the judge and pleading for assistance even though the judge did not respect people and did not believe in God. The judge ultimately decided to aid the woman because she had been persistent and had made numerous attempts to acquire assistance."

The essence of this story told by Jesus does not only to counsel you to "pray constantly and not lose heart" but also to keep trying. When you feel disheartened, be tenacious. When you feel like giving up, try once more and again. Continue to try and pray because victors never give up; losers never try.

Let's examine another example of perseverance that Jesus provided His disciples and identify some traits of those who are persistent.

Reading from the Bible: (*Luke 11:5-8*).

"Then He said to them, "Suppose one of you has a friend, and goes to him at midnight and says, 'Friend, lend me three loaves of bread, because a friend of mine on a journey has come to me, and I have nothing to set before him.' "Then the one inside answers, 'Don't bother me. The door is already locked, and my children are with me in bed. I can't get up and give you anything.' I tell you, though he will not get up and give him the bread because he is his friend, yet because of the man's boldness {or persistence} he will get up and give him as much as he needs."

This above scripture imparts a lesson on tenacity. The lesson here is how to persevere until every impediment is overcome. There are countless roadblocks, hazy solutions, unattainable options, challenging puzzles, challenging decisions, and unforeseen occurrences on your journey to greater heights, and one quality that you need to soar is to keep trying and be persistent.

Persistence is a sure way to get anything you want from others or from God; let us highlight some traits of persistent people; I hope to inspire you to be more persistent.

1. They don't accept excuses. As you can see from the paragraph above, the friend who was in bed provided excuses for why he couldn't help, but the friend who needed it kept asking. He refused to abandon his quest despite his many justifications. People with strong will do not give up easily.

Persistence places more importance on what it seeks than on what it hears. Many people frequently remark, "If only my father had lived, I would have advanced in life," or "If only my uncle in another country had assisted, my life wouldn't be like this." This is a thought of mediocrity. The bargain is that if you just keep trying, you'll succeed in making yourself proud. People attribute their shortcomings to past abuses (such as rape, molestation, etc.). Forget about the past and don't worry about the present; focus on the future, and you will lead a prosperous life.

2. They are patient and humble. Persistent people are like kids. They are understanding and modest. Jesus Christ said that to enter the kingdom of God; one must possess patience and humility. Nothing is too overwhelming to be accepted with this; patience and humility if the kingdom of God demands them. Children are adept at waiting and having faith. A small girl, who was four years old, waited for me to send her a balloon for two years. When she was four years old, I first promised her a balloon, and I only handed it to her when she was six. She kept waiting and asking for it while I kept forgetting and reiterating my vow. Children, unlike teenagers, will wait politely and ask questions. However, teenagers will slam the door in your face and call you a liar. Without humility and patience, persistence is a façade.

3. They are not egocentric. We can infer the reason for this brother's persistence from the verse above. For the benefit of another acquaintance, the brother demanded a favor from his bedtime companion. People who are persistent are not at all selfish because they have a compassionate heart. Persistent people know what it looks like to struggle, so they always help those in need.

4. They have a goal. Persistent people have goals, it is the achievement of this goal that makes them keep trying, and until they achieve the goal, they don't quit.

5. They are God's friends. Persistent people are considered to be God's friends because they can rely on God in any circumstance. They don't give up on God, and they don't let the wrong things cause them to compromise their faith. Waiting on God entails relying on and having faith in God in the face of life's ignorance. Persistent people soar like eagles, getting closer and closer to God.

They are unafraid. According to our text, this friend went to seek assistance at night. He continued with his goals, notwithstanding the night. Any individual can be paralyzed by fear, making it impossible to persist. If you wish to persevere and overcome all of life's obstacles, you must overcome the night, lightning, and thunderstorms. You don't need to be afraid to apply for that job, go to that interview, stay in that marriage, start that business again, join the ministry, or sit that exam once more. Rise up, throw your worries to the ground, and face your future!

DAY 29
KNOW YOUR VALUE

Too frequently, you measure your value on how others regard you, your success, or the ideal life you have led; the issue is that all those things are subject to change. If you base your value on how others treat you, you will feel devalued if they are wrong or let you down.

If you base your value on your accomplishments, earnings, the type of vehicle you drive, and the title that goes along with your name, then your value will decrease if something happens, and you are no longer in possession of these assets and titles. Some people don't feel good about themselves because they have made mistakes in life and aren't where they are expected to be; they now live insecurely and believe their value is based solely on their output.

Your value should simply be derived from the fact that you are a child of the Most High God, who breathed life into you. The way someone treats you has no bearing on how valuable you are; nothing they say or do can diminish who you are.

Your worth is not diminished by the errors you have made; those actions weren't indicative of who you are. You can improve your net worth by purchasing a larger home or a better vehicle, but doing so will not increase your value as a person. You were already valued even with a modest flat and no title to your name. Your new position may increase your influence but won't increase your value. You can be a stay-at-home mother raising your kids; even if you may not have the CEO's clout, you still have value.

Your value comes from your Creator; it is not based on what you do, what you create, or who you know; such things are merely surface-level and subject to change. You carry the DNA of the Almighty God, royalty, who breathed life into you. Eagles know that their value is in who they are, and since they know that their value lies in soaring, they are not intimidated by chicken crows.

Don't allow the enemy to diminish your value; he would prefer that you spend your life letting what others say make you feel inferior, comparing your life to theirs, and believing that you will feel good about yourself once you catch up to them, live in their area, perform flawlessly, or overcome the addiction. Nothing you do, accomplish, or overcome will increase your value; you already have value.

Put your shoulders back and start carrying yourself with confidence because God calls you a masterpiece, and you are one of a kind; you weren't mass-produced on an assembly line. You have been fearfully and wonderfully formed.

Let's talk about how Jesus Christ handled Himself with grace since He knew His value.

(St. Luke 4:1–3).

"Jesus, who was overflowing with the Holy Spirit, crossed the Jordan and followed the Spirit into the wilderness, where he encountered temptation from the devil for forty days. He didn't consume any food during those days, and he was famished. If you are the Son of God, transform this stone into bread, the devil cried to him."

The enemy attempted to diminish Jesus's value by focusing on his accomplishments and his capacity for miracles but noticed how Jesus responded.

(St. Luke 4:4), Jesus responded, "It is written, 'Man shall not live by bread alone."

In essence, Jesus was stating; I don't have to do anything to prove who I am, or perform to feel good about myself; I know who I am. The enemy attempted to convince Him to base His value on accomplishments and His ability to perform miracles; since He was unable to convince Him to do, He took another approach:

(St. Luke 4: 4-8)

"The devil took him to a vantage point and instantly displayed all of the world's kingdoms to him. He then told him, I will give you all of their power and majesty; it has been handed to me, and I may give it to anybody I choose. You can have it all if you worship me."

In response, Jesus said, "It is written: 'Worship the Lord your God and serve him only.'"

I don't need anything to show my value or worth, He was saying. I don't need to possess what you deem essential for me to feel good about who I am.

The enemy used another popular strategy to see if that would define Jesus' value.

(St. Luke 4:9–11)

"The devil took him to Jerusalem and forced him to stand atop the temple. He said, if you are the Son of God, throw yourself down from here. This is due to the passage that states, He will command his angels concerning you to guard you carefully; they will lift you up in their hands so that you will not strike your foot against a stone."

He was attempting to get Jesus to brag so that everyone would see and be amazed, and he would instantly become popular, but Jesus already knew who He was, the son of the living God, and didn't need anyone's approval to know that.

The adversary attempted to trick Jesus into demonstrating his identity. Many people constantly try to prove their importance or talent to others to feel good about themselves. It's a constant battle to outdo, out-perform, and out-dress others; realizing you don't need to prove anything or impress anyone is incredibly liberating. Relieving the pressure to compete, prove, or impress requires a lot of energy. If you are constantly trying to impress people, it can feel like you are on a treadmill; as soon as you have satisfied one person, another person will come along who you must satisfy. Get off the treadmill; there is nothing to prove.

Name brands are so valued in today's culture that you can become so covered with other names that you lose track of your own. You rely on all the well-known brands and independent labels to elevate your status. Owning things is OK, but don't let them define who you are or make you feel good about yourself.

You can increase your wardrobe and social circle, but that won't alter your value. Are you attempting to establish your worth and value by your network and appearance? Can you, like Jesus, say, "I don't need to be popular, have material things, or perform well; I am secure in who I am, who God made me to be" because in God is your true value.

DAY 30

BE A VISIONARY, DON'T GET DISTRACTED FROM FULFILLING YOUR VISION

Did you know that an eagle's vision is four to eight times more powerful than a human's? Small prey, like a rabbit, can be seen up to two miles away by them. However, as they descend, their vision adapts to focus on their prey as they get closer and closer. Amazing to have such a great and well-balanced vision!

The Bible likens Christians to eagles, and you can draw comparisons between some of the eagle's traits and what the Lord desires for His children to be.

(Psalm 103:5)

You give me everything I want and are wonderful to me. You've given my life a boost so that I can once more soar through the air like a soaring eagle!

Eagles are known for having strong eyesight and great vision. Despite his height, he has excellent vision and focus.

You are expected to understand both the large picture and the little intricacies as God's children. The Holy Spirit's revelation and the Word of God balance and correct your vision. You lose sight of God and what He wants to achieve in the grand scheme of things if you become overly focused on yourself and your immediate surroundings. Furthermore, crucial tasks for the Kingdom will go unfinished if you fail to recognize how God's bigger plan necessitates your cooperation with Him on a smaller scale. You really need to keep your vision and priorities in check.

The eagle's ability to see his prey and maintain constant focus on it, is crucial to his survival. In response, you must focus on your goal and avoid losing sight of it. It determines both your prosperity in this world and your ultimate life.

Eagles have a powerful, precise vision. They can locate their target and concentrate on it until they catch it. Similarly, an eagle can spot an enemy from a great distance and prevent him from coming close to and encroaching on its nest to harm its young.

Simply take your time and watch an eagle sitting or simply soaring above you. It keeps its body steady while maintaining a sideways head tilt to look for either a prey item or a predator.

Eagles can see their prey up to 10,000 feet away while flying at great heights. Fishing eagles can concentrate and find their food in both still and turbulent waters.

Having said that, it's critical to remember that great leaders have, do, and will continue to emerge. However, they have all shared the wonderful quality of being visionaries.

What is vision? Vision, which is the sense or capacity to see, is a crucial leadership attribute required to reach new heights.

Consider Martin Luther. Even at a time when everything was done based on skin color and pigmentation, he had the goal of a united America free from racial discrimination. He had every reason to give up, yet this vision gave him the will to continue his anti-racial crusades.

Nelson Mandela is another legend that exemplifies this. He arose, inspired by vision, to vehemently oppose apartheid at a time when it was the norm. Even after being imprisoned, his hope for a just and free South Africa remained unwavering. Because of this, when he was finally freed from the Robben Islands, he still had the fortitude to pardon his oppressors and continue his sincere anti-apartheid struggle.

You must have a vision that directs you toward a particular objective. Your vision must be broad but sharp, not hazy. Large yet fuzzy vision can be perplexing and may result in going in the wrong direction or achieving unintended objectives. However, a broad and narrowly focused vision will yield broad effects.

"We all live under the same sky, but we don't all have the same horizon." Words of Konrad Adenauer.

Dream big and look beyond! You have eyes like an eagle; focus on them. Step more quickly; you have the horse's limbs. You would defeat everything that burdens others on multiple occasions.

"Your vision will become clear only when you look into your heart. Who looks outside, and dreams? Who looks inside awakens." Words of Carl Jung.

Let the visionary in you arise, and let your vision becomes a reality!

DAY 31

WHO YOU ARE! IS WHO YOU ATTRACTS

The Law of Attraction states that you draw into your life whatever you are and focus on. If greatness is what you want, that is what you will continually attract, and the reverse is also true. Like attracts like is the true meaning of the Law of Attraction.

Whatever you focus your emotional attention and energy on will eventually return to you. You are reflected in the things and people you draw to yourself.

Does the question "Is the Law of Attraction real?" cross your mind frequently? Yes, that is the answer. Similar to gravity is the Law of Attraction. Every minute of every day, you witness it. It constantly has an effect on you and your life.

Focusing on unfavourable results and negative thoughts will cause you to attract them. You will materialize this if your thoughts are positive, your goals are clear, and you have a strategy. It is a vibration, not just an attraction. Positive vibrations will draw positive individuals to you and vice versa. You will not see an eagle clutch with a chicken; chickens clutch together because who you are is a vibration that brings you closer to whom you attract.

In the book of (*Philippians 4: 8*), *"Finally, brethren, whatsoever things are true, whatsoever things are honest, whatsoever things are of good report; if there be any virtue, and if there be any praise, think on these things."* Apostle Paul calls us to dwell on the things that are true, honourable, right, pure, lovely, of good repute, excellent and praiseworthy. We need to focus on good and honorable things in the world as opposed to the lies that Satan tries to weave into the world. We will attract it to our lives when we think about positive and healthy things.

Like attracts Like

Like attracts like is the simplest expression of the Law of Attraction. This implies that similar energy-based entities, objects, or individuals attract one another. Your energy shifts when you draw similar experiences, people, or things to you. Pleasant thoughts and feelings will draw pleasant circumstances or events. The opposite is also accurate. Negative things or events will come into your life because of your negative ideas and feelings.

Additionally, you will be drawn to things, people, or circumstances with energies like yours. It won't matter if the vibration is positive or negative; it will only strengthen it.

It's critical to keep in mind that thoughts manifest as things. Our world is shaped by the decisions we make and the ideas we have, and it is this world that we live in.

It is best to approach this with a clear intention since you will draw to you who you are. If you want to soar to greater heights, be mindful of your feelings, thoughts, and sensations. Spend time with people who inspire and impact you positively and who you want to develop into or become more like.

(Romans 8: 29), "God has predestined His people to conform to the image of His Son: that is, to become like Jesus." God wants His people to become like Christ. Christlikeness is the will of God for the people of God. The more we spend time in God's presence; we will become more like Christ and attract the things of Christ. We must be Christ-like in all areas of our lives.

If you know and think that you are worthy of good things, you will start acting in a certain way. Consciously, you will place yourself in situations that will lead you in the direction you need to go. According to the Law of Attraction, you get precisely what you think you deserve. More specifically, more of what you want and more of what you already know you are entitled to.

Your limiting ideas and sentiments that you don't deserve anything will have an impact on your behavior. You will act in a way that prevents you from being in situations that will result in any positive consequences. You will speak negatively or act unfavorably. It won't occur to you that the time is exact. You won't always be at the right place at the right moment. According to the Law of Attraction, you get precisely what you think you deserve. In other words, even though you know you don't deserve it, your actions actually result in you getting less of what you want.

CONCLUSION
YOU HAVE THE CHOICE TO CHOOSE

Whether to be an eagle or a chicken is one of many essential decisions you must make in life, although it is never really discussed. Throughout this inspiring book, we have established that eagles are fierce and soar high above the clouds with other eagles, whereas chickens scrape on the ground and loiter around with other chickens. Which one do you intend to become?

EAGLES

The granite block that the weak encountered as a barrier now serves as a steppingstone for the powerful. Theodore Carlyle This proverb accurately captures the distinction between eagles and chickens. Eagles view challenges as mere steppingstones on the path to their own achievement in assisting others and achieving their long-term objectives. When challenges arise, chickens tend to be weak, give up easily, and fail to persevere.

If you choose to be an eagle, you overcome difficulty alongside people who are similar to yourself and adapt to constantly changing situations. You stand up for what is right and don't let other people's viewpoints deter you from moving on and achieving your intended objectives. Since you know your value and worth, you grab life by the horns and don't care if you get hurt. You are a courageous, determined, and self-assured person.

You enlist the aid of others while being modest enough to acknowledge your own accomplishments without bragging. You overcome challenges and don't worry about what people think about you behind your back since you entirely believe in yourself. No matter who believes you deserve, you achieve your goals and help others along the way without giving any attention to praise. You treat rejection as a step toward a yes and refuse to accept no as an answer. You come up with solutions to people's issues, and then you act in a big way to put your amazing concepts into practice and use them for the greater good.

CHICKENS

Chickens don't live very long lives, but it seems like they like just plowing through it and wandering around aimlessly with other chickens. Chickens are not particularly successful because they give up too easily. Thomas Edison said it best: "Our greatest weakness lies in giving up." The best approach to achieving success is always to give something another shot.

Weak people and those who lack confidence in themselves decide to give up since their trip isn't significant enough to make the sacrifice, and it is tremendously difficult for them to find the steps to success.

People who are like chickens are afraid to try anything new or take risks. Chickens are easily side-tracked and always go for the simplest course of action. Chickens constantly make a lot of noise, yet they hardly ever get anything done. Because they give up before completing any task or important goal, chickens don't have a lot of self-esteem and let other chickens lead them away from their goal.

Chickens' minds are not favorably trained to compartmentalize their priorities, timetables, and tasks in order to make the most favorable use of their time. Chickens let other people's perceptions of them determine who they should be. Chickens get used to making do and developing a poor lifestyle.

Between eagles and chickens, there is a clear illustration of polar opposite character traits. Being an eagle is considerably more challenging because nothing worthwhile comes easily, but it will be worth it. You must decide whether you are an eagle or a chicken, and then you must create a vision for your future and fervently believe that vision will come true. You are born to soar, and the choice is in your hands.

YOU ARE BORN TO SOAR

You have the willpower within you to overcome and recover all. "Born to Soar" means more than just flying; it means rising swiftly above all odds. To rise above all obstacles, hurdles, circumstances, and challenges that, the enemy has laid into your path to limit you and stop you.

You are Born to Soar not snore! You were made to go above the normal levels; to go through life's barriers and go beyond your normal expectations. To do something you've never done before. You were created not to fly but to soar high like an eagle.

An eagle soars despite how they're feeling. It's time to soar like an eagle, break through limitations, and accomplish your true potential; instead of being stuck in a place of stagnancy. Where you are today is not permanent. God created you and anointed you, with wings like an eagle to accomplish all and soar higher than ever before in Jesus' name Amen.

9 789693 392265